THE NATURE OF NATURE

Why We Need the Wild

ENRIC SALA

Washington, D.C.

Published by National Geographic Partners, LLC
1145 17th Street NW Washington, DC 20036

COVER AND CHAPTER OPENER ILLUSTRATIONS: Spring Stories, Life in the Tropics, Tropical Desire, and Inhabitants of the Sea patterns © Piñata/www.youworkforthem.com.

PHOTO INSERT: 1, Jim Richardson/National Geographic Image Collection (NGIC); 2 (UP), Enric Sala; 2 (LO), Michael Nichols/NGIC; 3 (UP), Aleksander Bolbot/Shutterstock; 3 (LO), Fraser Hall/robertharding/NGIC; 4, Thomas P. Peschak/NGIC; 5 (BOTH), Octavio Aburto; 6-7, Science Source; 8 (UP), Mattias Klum/NGIC; 8 (LO), Konrad Wothe/Minden Pictures; 9 (UP), Norbert Rosing/NGIC; 9 (LO), Cagan H. Sekercioglu/NGIC; 10 (UP), NASA Goddard Space Flight Center Image by Reto Stôkli (land surface, shallow water, clouds). Enhancements by Robert Simmon (ocean color, compositing, 3D globes, animation). Data and technical support: MODIS Land Group; MODIS Science Data Support Team; MODIS Atmosphere Group; MODIS Ocean Group Additional data: USGS EROS Data Center (topography); USGS Terrestrial Remote Sensing Flagstaff Field Center (Antarctica); Defense Meteorological Satellite Program (city lights); 10 (LO), Brian Skerry/NGIC; 11 (UP), Xose Manuel Casal Luis/Alamy Stock Photo; 11 (LO), Cyril Ruoso/Minden Pictures; 12-13, Art: Beau Daniels. Sources: Suzanne Simard and Camille Defrenne, University of British Columbia; Kevin Beiler, Eberswalde University for Sustainable Development; 14 (UP), C.R. Burrell; 14 (LO), Tom Murphy/NGIC; 15, Colin Monteath/age fotostock; 16, Enric Sala.

ISBN: 978-1-4262-2101-9

Financially supported by the National Geographic Society.

Since 1888, the National Geographic Society has funded more than 13,000 research, exploration, and preservation projects around the world. National Geographic Partners distributes a portion of the funds it receives from your purchase to National Geographic Society to support programs including the conservation of animals and their habitats.

Get closer to National Geographic explorers and photographers, and connect with our global community. Join us today at nationalgeographic.com/join

For rights or permissions inquiries, please contact National Geographic Books Subsidiary Rights: bookrights@natgeo.com

Interior design: Melissa Farris and Nicole Miller

Printed in the United States of America

20/BVG-PCML/1

CONTENTS

Foreword by HRH The Prince of Wales.. 6
Introduction by Edward O. Wilson 9

1 RE-CREATING NATURE 11
2 WHAT'S AN ECOSYSTEM? 25
3 THE SMALLEST ECOSYSTEM 33
4 SUCCESSION.. 47
5 BOUNDARIES.. 63
6 ARE ALL SPECIES EQUAL?..77
7 THE BIOSPHERE 95
8 HOW ARE WE DIFFERENT? 111
9 DIVERSITY IS GOOD 129
10 PROTECTED AREAS 143
11 REWILDING.. 161
12 THE MORAL IMPERATIVE..179
13 THE ECONOMICS OF NATURE 191
14 WHY WE NEED THE WILD 209
Epilogue: THE NATURE OF CORONAVIRUS 223

Acknowledgments..239
Key References 241
Index 251

To all those who dedicate their lives
to preserve the diversity
and abundance of life on Earth

During the last forty years, I have had an opportunity to visit some of the most stunning places on Earth and seen the devastation caused by our over-exploitation of the natural world. We are in the midst of an existential crisis, not only affecting the survival of our very society, but also about our place in the world. Global warming, climate change and the destruction of biodiversity worldwide, caused by human activities, are the most dangerous threats that humanity has ever faced. At the same time, as we have replaced the wild with the domesticated, we have distanced ourselves from Nature. Long ago, we unilaterally decided to place ourselves *above* Nature, instead of acknowledging that we exist *within* Nature.

There is indeed a deep mutual interdependence within our natural world which is active at all levels, sustaining individual species so that the great diversity of life can flourish within the natural limits of the whole. We do not truly know how many species there are – we can only guess – and we still know less about what species do. But what we know is the greatest wonder we ever encountered. Plants and bacteria give us the oxygen we breathe, insects pollinate our crops and forests filter the water we drink, among many other critical services. Millions of species work together to produce a harmony that we cannot explain, but which works to sustain our world – and to keep ourselves alive and prosperous.

In the modern era, the sense of awe and wonder in the face of the works of Nature has been abandoned in favour of monetary value. Therefore, being able to show the economic value of Nature, of healthy ecosystems, is paramount. Economists have shown that the value provided in services by the natural world for free is larger than the global gross domestic product. Yet, at this moment, we have a hugely important opportunity to reimagine the world through the lens of a new global market and a new way to measure prosperity, with clear benefits to people and planet at the heart of value creation. This is why, in September 2019, in collaboration with the World Economic Forum, I created the Sustainable Markets Council with the goal of fostering the development of a new type of market: green, inclusive, equitable and profitable. I would like to emphasize that profitability in our new world ought to mean obtaining net benefits while restoring the natural world that is the foundation of our wealth.

But valuing the natural world through an economic lens is not enough. I also believe that we need to abandon our purely mechanistic and utilitarian approach to life and adopt a humbler attitude – in other words, to restore a sense of the sacred. Human prosperity and empathy and respect for all living creatures are not mutually exclusive; they can go hand in hand. In fact, that may be the key to our survival.

The good news is that we know what the solutions to the environmental crisis are. If we were to choose three main solutions, we need to phase out fossil fuels, change the way we produce food and protect more of Nature. For example, on the Duchy of Cornwall's Home Farm in Gloucestershire, I have been able to shift from chemically-dependent farming to organic, agro-ecological production methods, where fertility is sustained by plants, animals and careful management that includes rotation of the land. Instead of an exploitative relationship with Nature, the farm works in partnership with Nature. Scaling such efforts globally could restore the fertility of the soil, produce healthier food, and in turn absorb huge amounts of our carbon pollution.

I am delighted to be able to contribute this foreword for Dr. Enric Sala's *The Nature of Nature* because his book touches on all these points. Enric's book tells stories of discovery of key ecological principles that go beyond facts and data. There is fascination and love in the discovery of how Nature works. A deep appreciation of natural history is a kind of poetry, which should instil a sense of wonder. And that leads to love of the world of which we are an intrinsic part, with a profound respect for the existence of other creatures. The only way forward is to reconnect with Nature and restore vital eco-systems so that our life support system – and the engine of the human economy – can continue supporting us and the rest of life on the planet.

INTRODUCTION

I N THIS COMPELLING NEW BOOK, *The Nature of Nature—Why We Need the Wild,* Enric Sala takes us on a guided tour of Earth's marine environment, this time not only its aesthetic power but also the life-giving products of Earth's majority living cover. The health of the sea, no less than the health of the land, is ultimately responsible for every morsel we put in our mouths, every breath of air we take. We cannot create the land and sea, but we can destroy them.

It is fortunate that we humans can fully appreciate nature, even though through science we have only begun to understand her. What exactly is she, this Mother Nature, that we should give her almost divine status? I have devoted a large part of my life as an ecologist to the scientific study of nature, yet a definition of it in words still escapes me and most others I challenge. Nature evokes a feeling as much as a physical image. So let me try a definition that is more poetry than science.

Nature, sometimes called Mother Nature, is the metaphorical goddess of everything in the universe beyond human control, from the sweet descent of her sunsets to the tantrums of her thunderstorms; from the explosive brilliance of her ecosystems to the black void of her empty space.

Sala's approach to marine biology, aside from the beauty of his photographs, lies in the clarity of his vision of marine ecology as a scientific vision comparable to that achieved by studies of terrestrial ecology. The convergence is especially striking in the origin and evolution of ecosystems to land habitats such as forest and grassland on the one hand and coral reefs and other marine habitats on the other. Ecosystems, with their enormous origami-like relationships, are among the most complex of all natural constructions. To understand the patterns and laws of their common origins is one of the most important challenges of science in the present century. *The Nature of Nature* can help us in that quest.

—Edward O. Wilson

CHAPTER ONE

RE-CREATING NATURE

O N SEPTEMBER 26, 1991, eight people (four men and four women) were locked in a closed facility the size of two soccer fields in Oracle, Arizona. The project was called Biosphere 2, and its goal was to conduct an experiment to test whether we can build a viable self-sustaining human colony. The real biosphere—what one could call Biosphere 1—is the self-sustaining web of life that forms the thin living skin of our planet and makes our life possible. If Biosphere 2 succeeded, it would pave our way to colonizing other planets.

The plan was to create a simplified model of our biosphere that could sustain the lives of eight humans. Within a futuristic-looking glass and stainless steel structure, developers re-created a rainforest, a fog desert, a thorn-scrub, a savanna, a marsh, a mangrove, and a coral reef—together with an agricultural area where the participants could grow their food. These habitats were hermetically isolated from the world outside and designed based on the best ecological knowledge. But things started to go wrong rather quickly.

After 16 months, the oxygen concentration in Biosphere 2 had dropped from the healthy 21 percent in our atmosphere to a low 14 percent—low enough that some "biospherians" showed symptoms of altitude sickness. The soils imported into the enclosure were very rich in organic matter, selected with the goal of producing enough nutrients for vegetation to grow over time. As it turned out, though, microbes in the soil processed that organic matter, sucking up oxygen and building up carbon dioxide (CO_2). At the same time, the plants being grown were not large enough to produce enough oxygen to compensate or to absorb that extra CO_2. In addition, that extra CO_2 reacted with the concrete in the structure, forming calcium carbonate, which meant that carbon and oxygen were not available to the living beings in the enclosure anymore. In the long run, oxygen had to be pumped into the experiment to keep the system and its inhabitants alive.

One of the biggest problems within the enclosure was the rise in CO_2—a prophetic consequence, since rising levels of CO_2 represent one of the major threats to human civilization on the planet today. But not only the atmosphere failed in Biosphere 2—the wildlife did too. Species became extinct faster than anticipated, and few of the introduced animals survived the experiment. The ecological designers had brought in bees, moths, butterflies, and hummingbirds as pollinators. They had also included snakes, skinks, lizards, turtles, and bats, among other vertebrates. But the bees and hummingbirds died off, meaning that plants could no longer reproduce by themselves. Meanwhile, other species boomed, including crazy ants, cockroaches, and morning glories, which managed to overgrow every other plant. Thus, the biospherians had to spend over half of their time just tending to their crops. Only six out of 25 small vertebrate species survived by the end of the experiment.

The first mission of Biosphere 2 ended two years after it started. A second mission in 1994 only lasted six months, mostly because of human conflict: Some biospherians insisted on opening up air locks, and a bitter dispute between the main financer of the project and the in-site management team resulted in federal marshals ousting the team by serving a restraining order.

What did we learn from Biosphere 2? Some biospherians say that the experiment was a success because it taught them to become self-sufficient and to solve unexpected problems. There is some truth to that. Given more time, maybe the enclosed habitat could have become self-sustaining—likely different from what the designers of Biosphere 2 envisioned, but a functioning ecosystem none-theless. The fact is, in the two years of the first mission, Biosphere 2 did not turn into slime.

Moreover, this is the way science advances. We experiment, fail, learn from it, and try new things using the knowledge we acquire. We tend to learn more from our failures than from our successes. Biosphere 2 was a bold, innovative experiment that taught us very bluntly how difficult it is to maintain a relatively simple ecosystem and a healthy atmosphere. It failed to replicate the viability of Earth for human life. The experiment was a testament to our ignorance of how life on our planet works—and our inability to re-create it.

In essence, what it did show is that our planet is a miracle. It does not matter whether you believe Earth was created by an omniscient God, or grown by physical forces from cosmic dust circling around a nascent star, or generated as a computer simulation (yes, there is a group of theoretical physicists who believe so). We're traveling in a spaceship 107,800 kilometers an hour (67,000 mph) around a star that is in turn traveling 69,200 kilometers an hour (43,000 mph) in the suburban part of our galaxy. There are 400 billion planets in our galaxy alone, orbiting around at least 100 billion stars. What makes Earth truly unique is life. Life on Earth and its mind-blowing, intertwining complexity is the greatest miracle humanity has known.

But if we had to make a catalog of all that we know about the living creatures on Earth, 99 percent of the pages would be blank. To date, scientists have described fewer than two million species of multicellular organisms—the plants and animals we can see. We know the birds pretty well. We also know the mammals, fish, corals, and flowering plants well, even though every year we add a total of 6,000 new species to our catalog. But scientists estimate that the total number of species is probably around nine million. This does not include single-cell organisms, the microbes such as bacteria and archaea, found everywhere from our guts to the clouds above us to two miles underground. These could add up to a trillion species to the census, yet we have come to know only a fraction of them.

But one thing we know with absolute certainty is that everything we need to survive—every morsel of food we put in our mouths, the oxygen in every breath we take, the clean water we drink—is the product of work done by other species. They give us so much, and how do we repay them? We ignore, undo, and destroy them.

We are erasing species from existence at a rate a thousand times faster than the natural extinction rate. A 2019 United Nations report warned that human activities will drive the extinction of one million species of plants and animals (one in nine) in the next few decades. And we're filling the void—actually, creating that void—by replacing that lost diversity of life with our food sources. Today, 96 percent of the mass of mammals on the land is us and our domesticated livestock. Only 4 percent is everything else, from elephants to bison to panda bears. As a matter of fact, we have lost 60 percent of the terrestrial wildlife since 1970 and 90 percent of the large fish in the ocean (sharks, tuna, cod) in the last century. Seventy percent of the birds on Earth are our domesticated poultry—mostly chickens—and only 30 percent are wild.

Not only are we replacing thousands of species of wildlife with a few species of farm animals, but we're also transforming the land at a scale second only to the forces of plate tectonics. Presently, more than half of the inhabitable land surface is farmed or pastured—gone are the former forests and grasslands that used to enrich those soils—and almost 80 percent of that agricultural land is used to raise or feed livestock.

If we continue our ways, soon the only large animals left on the planet will be us, our domesticated food, and our pets, and the largest plant communities won't be the magnificent tropical and boreal forests, but monocultures like the vast industrial croplands that now make up the American Midwest. Is this a viable future for humanity? Can we survive on a planet without wild places? If worse comes to worst, will we be able to build viable colonies on other planets that can support a self-sustaining human society?

Biosphere 2 was carried out 25 years ago. Our science and technology has improved phenomenally since then. In fact, as of November 2000, humans did become the long-term residents of a space colony: the International Space Station (ISS). The ISS is a miracle of engineering that orbits Earth at an average altitude of 409 kilometers (254 mi). It is the only existing human colony in space—but still attached to our planet by its gravitational pull, like the infant who does not dare to wander too far from mother. It takes an extremely complex international cooperation, with control centers in the United States, Canada, France, Germany, Russia, and Japan, to keep between two and eight astronauts alive up there. In addition to its initial price tag of a hundred billion dollars, it costs NASA alone three billion dollars every year to cover its share of running the ISS. That means ensuring that those few people have, at the very least, a stable supply of oxygen to breathe, water to drink, and food to eat—plus a protective shield against cosmic radiation and the lethal void. In space, everything is trying to kill you. If we learned one thing from Biosphere 2, or from the daily work necessary to keep humans in the ISS alive, it is that we should worship our actual biosphere that keeps us alive.

Here on Earth, we don't have to worry about cosmic radiation. (Have you ever met anyone who does?) We don't have to worry about—or pay anything for—the oxygen we breathe. Until recently, many of us did not have to pay anything for the water we drink—it fell from the sky or arose from eternal springs. In addition, we underpay for our food, because we are not charged for the sunlight that keeps plants going or for the bees that pollinate our orchards—or, until recently, for the environmental costs created by our industrial food production processes.

If it's so difficult to keep even small ecosystems stable enough to sustain the life of a handful of humans, how do nine million species of plants and animals and a trillion species of microbes coexist and allow for our survival? How does this Biosphere 1 manage to keep everything alive and in balance? In what way do we depend on all those other species for our own survival?

This book aims to answer these questions.

I HAVE SPENT the last 30 years studying natural ecosystems, mostly those in the ocean. These questions have been in my mind since I began studying biology in college in 1986, and I have dedicated a great part of my life to try to make sense of the overwhelming miracle of life on Earth.

I started my forays into marine biology as an undergraduate, studying the marine algae that grew on the rocky shores of the Costa Brava in Catalonia, Spain. First, I had to identify them—that is, I needed to know which species was which, in the same way that any botanist should be able to distinguish an oak from a pine. On the coast of Catalonia alone there are more than 500 different species of algae, so this was no easy task. Before the internet, the only source of identification were monographs published in specialized journals that were available either at the university library or, more often, in the private libraries of a handful of professors who were students of algae. Fortunately for me, one of them, Lluís Polo, became my professor of botany during my second year of biology studies at the University of Girona, in my hometown.

During the summer months I worked the night shift at my uncle's restaurant on the beach. After the latest diners left (and in the Mediterranean summer, that meant after midnight), I had to reconcile the receipts and reload the bar fridges. When all my co-workers had gone back home or were partying at one of the local discotheques, I was carrying cases of sodas, beer, and sparkling water from the pantry in the back of the restaurant to the bar near the entrance. I typically closed the doors of the restaurant after 1 a.m. and went to bed, exhausted. But I never slept well because of the excitement I felt about the coming day. I knew I needed to wake up early to get to the water before the hordes of summer tourists colonized the coves nearby.

Shortly after 8 a.m., I walked by closed restaurants, yet-to-be-opened stores selling beach accessories and perfumes, and open yet sleepy newspaper stands. I carried a mesh bag containing my mask, snorkel, fins, a blunt kitchen knife, an old pair of pantyhose, and a beach towel. Walking down steps cut into the rock, I meandered among curvy orange and pinkish rocks crowned by green pines that curled toward the Mediterranean, as though they were bowing to the sea. At the base of the steps were little sandy coves, hugged by the rocky promontories. The small waves of the calm morning sea kissed the beach with a hush of such regularity that, had I lain on the sand for a minute, they would have put me to sleep. But instead I jumped into the clear turquoise waters with the knife and the pantyhose, on my quest for algae, as many different types as possible, always looking for those I had never seen before. That was my little paradise.

Two days a week I would take the 8 a.m. bus to Girona, 36 kilometers (22 mi) from the beach, to visit Polo at his laboratory. He was the one who introduced me to the wonderful world of algae. First I learned to divide the algae between three evident groups: brown, red, and green. But some algae that looked brown actually belonged with the red algae. Scratching my head, I started to realize that things might not be so evident in nature as one might think. The diversity of species was astounding: brown algae that looked like foot-long Christmas trees, green algae like little lettuce only two cells thick, and minute red algae no thicker than a human hair that, under the microscope, revealed branches that divided in perfect symmetry with alternating bands of red and transparent cells. In its algae, the Mediterranean was as diverse as any exotic coral reef, only at a miniature scale. Another local expert who later became my mentor and one of my closest friends, Enric (Kike) Ballesteros, once took a sample at 40 meters (131 ft) deep and identified 149 different types of algae in an area the size of a cafeteria tray.

Very quickly I realized that these algae were not found just anywhere. Each kind had its own favored location. Some algae grew on top of each other, sometimes with algae growing on algae growing on algae. And the algae at the base might grow on a rock or over a barnacle or mussel. There was a regularity: Different species—and the distinct "communities" they formed—were found at different depths, at different exposures to waves, and at different exposures to light (for example, on top of an underwater boulder versus at the edge of a rock overhang). Polo and Ballesteros taught me that these algal communities form distinct belts found at predictable depths. Some algae—the little Christmas trees—were only present at the interface between the rocks and the sea, in rough areas exposed to the waves, because that was the only place where they escaped from the schools of voracious salema porgies, a species of sea bream with an oblong silver body with golden stripes (which, by the way, can cause hallucinations when eaten). Other algae grew abundantly on top of underwater boulders. They didn't need the protection of rough waves or rocky overhangs because they produced chemical compounds that made them unpalatable to the fish.

As I sorted algae in the lab, I discovered thousands of little creatures living among their branches—crabs, shrimplike amphipods, wood lice, worms, snails, sea slugs, and many more. Some of these species were eating the algae, some were eating each other, and all were hiding from the fish within the algal canopy. The more I learned, the more new worlds appeared in front of my eyes. My mind was ever hungry, and marine biology became my life and my passion.

FAST-FORWARD 10 YEARS. After finishing my Ph.D., I moved to the prestigious Scripps Institution of Oceanography in La Jolla, California. As a university professor, my job was to educate the future leaders in the field of marine ecology and conservation, to conduct scientific research, and to publish in scientific journals. But the places that I was studying, places that I loved deeply, were falling under the force of the relentless human sledgehammer. Corals and sea-grasses were dying everywhere, and fish were being taken out of the water faster than they could reproduce. What had been lush underwater gardens full of large animals were being turned into dead reefs overgrown by brown algae and murky jellyfish dystopias.

One day I realized that all I was doing was just writing the obituary of ocean life. In fact, many of my colleagues and I were *rewriting* the obituary with more and more precision. I felt like the doctor telling you how you are going to die with excruciating detail, but without offering a cure.

That's when I decided to quit academia and dedicate my life to reversing the degradation of the ocean. Thus, I have spent the last 12 years as a National Geographic explorer-in-residence, helping to protect some of the last wild places in the ocean through our Pristine Seas project. Visiting these places has allowed our team to catch glimpses of intact, fully functioning ecosystems. I have dived, explored, and conducted research in many places around the world, from the polar regions to temperate seas to the tropics. I have seen degraded places, pristine places, and many in between. I have seen the miraculous recovery of overfished places once fishing stopped. I have seen nature thrive in places, and nature wane in others. I have been privileged to witness what few people have, and I understand, from the purely rational to the supremely spiritual level, why we need all these species around us.

It all started with my being able to tell species apart, to know who all my new friends were. Then came observing who lives next to whom, how, and where. Then who eats whom. And, more recently, recognizing the impact of human activity on the natural world.

The Nature of Nature explores how the natural world works, outlines the consequences of its unraveling by our activities, and offers practical solutions—with a description of societal and economic benefits. The next 10 chapters of this book are a step-by-step crash course in ecology—you might call it "ecology for people in a hurry": what species do, how they coexist, and how the natural world self-assembles and works, compared with our human-built environment— with implications on how to run our society and economy more efficiently. What I am offering is a mix of my own first-hand experience and stories of science heroes, some of whom I have been privileged to know and work with. In Chapter 12 I discuss the moral case for the conservation of life on Earth, because utility cannot be the only lens through which we see the world. In other words: Do other creatures have a right to exist, and why? In Chapter 13 I explain why it makes economic sense to protect more of the natural world than to degrade it.

Chapter 14 synthesizes the lessons from the book and proposes practical solutions for safeguarding our biosphere and human society at the same time. I thought this was going to be the last chapter. But after the book had been edited and was ready for printing, the COVID-19 pandemic happened. My editors and I decided to delay the production process so I could write a final section on the novel coronavirus, which has turned out to be the most powerful wake-up call to the world about the enormous risks to human health posed by our broken relationship with nature.

By talking to the brain and the heart, and at the same time reaching into the pocket, I hope to illuminate an inner appreciation for all life on Earth, instill a greater sense of humility, and help us understand why we need a world with wild places.

CHAPTER TWO

WHAT'S AN ECOSYSTEM?

C ORSICA, the granite island in the middle of the western Mediterranean, is one of my favorite places on Earth. When I first went to conduct research there as part of my Ph.D. work, in 1993, it was, as my doctoral adviser Charles-François Boudouresque warned me, "like traveling back to the Mediterranean of 500 years ago."

I had spent my childhood summers in coastal towns with crowded beaches and concrete walls. Even my favorite coves, where I did my first observations of marine life, were surrounded by villas, hotels, and apartment blocks. But Corsica was different. It was just before sunrise when the ferry that took me from mainland France approached the shoreline of Ajaccio, in the southwest of the island. I stood on deck, sleepy but in awe. The tall and proud Corsica was wild, with very few signs of human habitation, in contrast with the mainland I was used to, where patches of green poked through concrete and asphalt. As the sun peeked over the mountains, a pocket of warm air delivered an aroma from the island that filled my eyes with tears. I can still remember it: juniper, laurel, rosemary, myrtle, sage, mint, thyme, and lavender—the essence of the wild maquis of Corsica. That was the beginning of a love affair that soon became central to my scientific endeavors.

I am extremely privileged to have been to Corsica many times with a handful of dear friends and colleagues, to conduct scientific research at the Scandola Marine Reserve, on the northwest side of the island. Many people have joined us over the years, but initially we were a tight group of friends, people who also were my mentors and colleagues: Kike Ballesteros, who taught me about algae and natural history; Mikel Zabala, an amazing naturalist and professor of ecology at the University of Barcelona who co-directed my Ph.D. thesis; and Joaquim Garrabou, also working on his Ph.D. at the time, studying how the dynamics of ecological communities change with depth. What brought us together was that we were all fanatic divers fascinated by nature, and all of us were unable to stay idle. We all wore green wet suits for diving and, bouncing off the nickname for the famous U.S. basketball team that won the Olympic title in Barcelona in 1992, we called ourselves the "green team."

Our fieldwork in Corsica typically took place in October, after the few tourists were gone and the reserve manager could dedicate his attention to our work. October in Corsica is a crapshoot. You never know what weather you will get. Some years we had sun and calm seas, but other years we had strong winds or rough seas that prevented us from reaching our diving spots. But we never stood idle, and when the sea did not want us, we explored the old oak forests in search of wild mushrooms—mostly the delicious cèpes, chanterelles, and Caesar's mushrooms. Or we simply walked the elegant pine forests along the desert beaches, or hiked the spectacular granite mountains that stretch up to their summit at Monte Cintu, 2,710 meters (8,891 ft) above sea level.

IF WE PUT TOGETHER all the dives and hikes in one transect from depths to heights, it would reveal a clear distribution of Corsica's plants and animals. Sixty meters (197 ft) below the surface are forests of white and red sea fans and yellow sponges like organ pipe cactus. At 50 meters (164 ft) they give way to a forest of old brown algae that look like miniature olive trees, with gnarled trunks and a tuft of branches growing from what look like olive pits. As we move toward the surface, a different species of brown alga appears at about 30 meters (98.5 ft) depth, this one with a brown trunk as thick as a thumb, crowned by a palm tree–like canopy. Different algal species become more dominant closer to the surface, forming forests of different height and age. The animals follow similar patterns, with sea fans living deeper and sea urchins closer to the surface. Some fish, such as the salema porgy, move through different depths, but most species are found within a predictable range.

As we exit the water, we climb red volcanic rocks sprinkled with deep-green bushes and the wild aromatic herbs that brought me to tears when I first smelled them—and still fill me with sweet nostalgia every time I recall them. Or we can turn left and walk across a sandy beach bordered with stone pines, cork oak, and evergreen oak, and meet an undammed river, home to freshwater turtles and fringed by a riparian forest. As we climb up, we encounter maritime pine interspersed with mixed forests of downy oak, sessile oak, Italian alder, and sweet chestnut, with a rich diversity of the wild mushrooms that we gathered and enjoyed when the weather was too rough for diving. Higher up on the mountain, these broadleaf deciduous forests are replaced by forests of Corsican pine on the slopes facing south, and silver fir and European beech on the slopes facing north. Above the forest line, at about 2,000 meters (6,560 ft), we find shrublands of green alder, juniper, sycamore, maple, and silver birch. Continuing up, eventually it becomes too cold for large plants, and all you can see are lichens growing stoically on granite. The very top of Monte Cintu is bare rock—and a lot of snow in the winter.

If we drew the borders between the different types of plant and animal associations we saw, they would look like a series of belts, roughly parallel to each other. Each of these unique groupings of plants and animals can also be defined as different ecological systems—or ecosystems.

AN ECOSYSTEM is simply the community of living organisms (microbes, plants, and animals) and the physical environment (the habitat) they occupy. The organisms and their relationships are what ecologists call a "food web"—a collage of overlapping food chains where a predator eats a predator eats a prey, and where species compete for space, light, and other resources. But living beings don't just occupy their habitat, be it granite or volcanic rock, sandy beaches or inland plains; they can actually create their own habitat (for example, coral reefs) and provide room and food for many creatures. If life on Earth is a miracle, what life does is still an even more wondrous miracle.

Ecosystems grow and shrink and senesce, and parts of them regress to a young state that allows dormant species to have a day in the sun. Ecosystems are never static. They self-regulate through feedback loops within the biological community but also between living organisms and their habitat. They create rain and regulate the weather. They fill the atmosphere with a mix of gases that allows us to breathe and survive. They filter the clean water we drink. They protect us from floods. They have been saving us from catastrophic climate change for more than a century. But few of us have noticed.

Ecosystems have had billions of years to experiment and, through trial and error, self-organize into the most efficient machines in the universe. They are always changing, and until recently they always fluctuated within reasonable bounds, following predictable pathways. We cannot really re-create much of what ecosystems do for us. Yet dead ecosystems have allowed humans to be the masters of life on our planet—and its destroyers too. But we will park all these stories for later.

Not only forests and wetlands and rivers are ecosystems. Our cities are too. For instance, New York City's habitat is primarily a built environment made of asphalt, concrete, glass, and steel, interspersed by some greenery. When thinking of wildlife in New York City, most may think of rats, Central Park squirrels, or the odd peregrine falcon nesting on the roof of an office building and making headlines. But New York is also home to thousands of plant and animal species that coexist with the city's almost nine million people. This wildlife includes coyotes, squirrels, bats, skunks, opossums, red foxes, white-tailed deer, snapping turtles, eastern box turtles, salamanders, and more than 200 species of birds. Strikingly, in the waters surrounding New York City, and in the Hudson River, live 80 species of fish. Even humpback whales and fin whales have been observed. In the most claustrophobic concrete jungle, life hangs on.

If humans suddenly abandoned New York City, the built habitat would collapse. New York City is like Emmentaler cheese belowground, with dozens of tunnels, 245 miles of subway routes, and 6,600 miles of sewer mains and pipes. Without the 290 pump rooms working 24/7 that the city currently uses to drain more than 16,000 gallons per minute of water from the Hudson River, the East River, and the Upper Bay, the metro routes and the tunnels would be flooded. That would turn the holes in the cheese even larger and eventually cause the collapse of buildings. It would not take long for dust to accumulate in holes and crevices on the surface, and for plants to colonize the rubble. Wildlife would start to overtake the ramshackle surroundings.

Life—and the ecosystems it forms—has an extraordinary capacity to regenerate and self-assemble, even in the most unlikely places. Everyone in my generation can remember the explosion of the Chernobyl nuclear reactor in 1986. Despite the heroic efforts of Soviet scientists, soldiers, and miners to contain the radiation, it became so pervasive that people were evacuated from the neighboring town of Pripyat—permanently. Even pets had to be killed to prevent them from spreading radiation. And then nature took over. Now the buildings are crumbling, conquered by shrubs and trees, and the city is the territory of wolves. Apparently the built habitat cannot survive without its builders. In a few thousand years, Pripyat might look like Maya cities in the jungle when first rediscovered under a thick canopy of green.

IF WE ZOOMED OUT from the Corsican forests, we would see the divide between the land and the sea. Zooming farther out, we'd notice that Corsica is an island ecosystem surrounded by the Mediterranean. Zooming farther out still, the Mediterranean itself would appear as a distinct ecosystem with clear boundaries north—the Alps and the Carpathian Mountains—and south—the Sahara. Astronauts on the International Space Station, who have zoomed out even farther, recognize that the entire planet is an ecosystem, with no visible borders except for those between land and sea, desert and vegetation, cities and farms. No wonder. Ecosystem comes from the ancient Greek word *oikos*, meaning "family," and also "house."

Full circle.

But how does this living miracle work and sustain itself? How can nine million species of creatures we can see and a trillion types of microbes we cannot see interact in a way that provides stability to the entire planet? To answer these questions, we need to start from the beginning. Let's put two species together and see what happens.

CHAPTER THREE

THE SMALLEST ECOSYSTEM

I N 1934, a Soviet biologist only 23 years old published a book titled *The Struggle for Existence*. This little book, unknown to most students of biology today, is one of the most important studies in the history of biology, for it provided the first experimental basis for understanding how species compete with each other and how species can destroy each other (and themselves) in a world of limited resources.

Georgyi Frantsevich Gause, that young biologist, was the son of Frants Gause, a professor of architecture, and Galina Gause, an industrial worker at an automotive steel plant. Gause and his family took long summer vacations to the Caucasus, where he developed a love for nature. At 17 he entered the prestigious Moscow State University. The Russian system required a faculty adviser for every student, and in one of those serendipitous moments that randomly shape a life and its influence in history, Gause was assigned to Professor Vladimir Alpatov.

Alpatov was influenced by American research on population growth, which hypothesized that the growth of any population, including humans, tends to slow as its density increases. That suggested that the human population would not grow forever until we exhausted all resources on the planet and died. Instead, the population would grow slowly in the beginning, then increase very fast, and then level off, and population numbers would stabilize. Biologists have observed this pattern of slow growth followed by explosive growth and finally stabilization—called logistic growth—in many a species since, including ourselves. It's the theory behind the prediction that the human population will likely stabilize around nine or 10 billion people by 2050.

In science, after a theory is proposed, it has to be tested with field observations or, ideally, with experiments. Gause thought that fieldwork would never be able to test these logistic growth assumptions properly because species do not live in a vacuum, since they are all interacting in a complex web of relationships. Simply put, there are too many confounding factors in nature to isolate the factors needed to test this hypothesis. But Gause thought that he could conduct experiments in the laboratory by building simplified environments, controlling all factors. Thus he started one of the most significant studies in the history of biology.

GAUSE WAS STRONGLY INFLUENCED by Charles Darwin, who had published his *On the Origin of Species* only a few decades earlier. Darwin assumed that all species compete in the struggle for existence in ways that we do not comprehend because of our ignorance of "the mutual relations of all organic beings." Darwin thought that "each organic being is striving to increase in a geometrical ratio; that each, at some period of its life, during some season of the year, during each generation, or at intervals, has to struggle for life and to suffer great destruction."

The "geometrical" growth (also called exponential growth) that Darwin mentioned means *explosive* growth. A great example to illustrate geometric growth is the tale of a craftsman who presented a chessboard to an Indian king. The king, marveled by the board and the game, offered the man any reward he wanted. The man asked that a single grain of rice be placed on the first square of the chessboard, then two grains in the second square, four in the third, eight in the fourth, and so on and so forth, doubling the number of grains in each new square until all 64 squares had been filled. That was the reward he requested, and the king agreed to it. But there was a little problem: When you double the amount of rice 64 times and add up all the rice grains found on all squares, it equals 210 billion metric tons, enough to bury all of India under one meter of rice.

Put another way, if every species were to increase geo-metrically—which could seem plausible, if every individual had just two babies—our planet would be filled with an enormous number of individuals of every species. But this is not what we see in our world. Instead, we see that not all species are equally abundant. In the African plains, grasses are more abundant than acacia trees, and wildebeests are more abundant than elephants. Thus Darwin thought that, despite every species' drive to reproduce as much as possi-ble, there must be something that keeps their abundances in check, some kind of "struggle for existence" that limits their growth. Part of that struggle is, of course, how much food is available. Another part of the struggle, Darwin thought, must be the relationship of each species with other species in the ecosystem.

Before Darwin's time, no one really understood how species interact with one another to form ecosystems. Biol-ogists knew that plants compete for light and soil nutrients, and that predators reduce the abundance of their prey, but they did not understand how species abundances stabilize within the web of complex relations. Gause wanted to prove that the complex relationships between organisms are deter-mined by simple processes that could be modeled mathe-matically. He wrote: "Such an elementary process is that of one species devouring another, or when there is a competi-tion for a common place between a small number of species in a limited microcosm."

A few years earlier, Umberto D'Ancona, an Italian biologist, conducted a statistical study on the numbers of fish sold in three markets in the northern Adriatic Sea. He observed that during World War I the relative numbers of predatory fish—sharks, rays, and skates—had increased relative to the smaller fish they feed on, and then decreased shortly after. He proposed that the drastic decline in fishing during the war had restored "the natural balance" of the marine ecosystem, whereas the intense fishing occurring after war's end had disturbed it. Unaware of the ecological explanation, D'Ancona asked his uncle, the famous mathematician Vito Volterra (by then retired), if he could come up with a mathematical model explaining his observations. Volterra quickly developed the first models for interactions between species. These models became the basis for understanding the relations between species that compete for a resource and the relations between predators and their prey. Applied to the Adriatic in the early 1900s, the model suggested that the decline in fishing allowed the large fish—the predators—to recover from human exploitation. More numerous predators ate more of their fish prey, hence the observed increase in the relative abundance of the predators. After the war, fishing resumed and predator numbers were depleted once more, which brought prey numbers up again.

Gause knew about D'Ancona's and Volterra's work, and he set out to test Volterra's models with experiments. Laboratories in the early 1900s tended to be quite archaic compared with what university students can enjoy today, but Gause's creativity compensated for the lack of resources. He created the microcosms he had envisioned using test tubes filled with food (a nutritive medium) and stopped with cotton wool. Within each glass tube was a self-contained ecosystem, isolated from all the confounding factors that one finds in nature.

GAUSE'S FIRST EXPERIMENT was intended to test whether a single species would grow following the logistical law. The species of choice was *Paramecium caudatum,* a single-celled organism the shape of a short cigar whose pointy end has not been cut. Its transparent body is covered with fine hairlike filaments that it uses to move and feed on small organisms such as bacteria and yeast. *Paramecium* is only 200–300 microns in size (a 20th the size of a medium rice grain), and it reproduces rapidly by dividing itself in two daughter cells, without need for sex with other individuals. That makes *Paramecium* an ideal organism for experiments involving multiple generations.

Gause introduced five individual *Paramecium* into small test tubes, each containing 0.5 cubic centimeter of nutritive medium (the equivalent of 10 drops of water). For six days he counted the number of individuals in every tube. The numbers increased rapidly in the beginning and more slowly later, until on the fourth day the *Paramecium* had reached an average abundance of 375 individuals per tube, attaining what Gause called the "saturating population." The growth of *Paramecium* in the microcosms fitted the logistical curve beautifully.

The next step was to complicate that mini-ecosystem one notch, by adding a second species. Gause believed that different species, no matter how closely related they are on the tree of life, do not use the environment in the same way. For instance, they must consume different quantities of food and excrete different quantities of metabolic products. His question was, Would two species living together reach a saturating population equal to the one they reached when living in isolation? Or would one species be victorious over the other—that is, reach a higher abundance?

Gause shifted to two species of yeast that ate the same food to assess the competition between them: *Saccharomyces cerevisiae,* the yeast used for brewing beer, and *Schizosaccharomyces kefir,* the yeast used to produce kefir. Both species can grow with or without oxygen. When yeasts grow without oxygen, fermentation occurs: They create ethanol as a waste product. When oxygen is added to the mix, some fermentation still occurs, but yeast cells divide more rapidly. Both species produce alcoholic fermentation, but the kefir yeast grows very slowly without oxygen.

First Gause grew each species in isolation, to determine their saturating populations. Then he grew them together in the same test tube with a nutritive medium containing 5 percent sugar. He developed 111 separate microcosms for this experiment, and then averaged the results across three treatments: beer yeast growing alone, kefir yeast growing alone, and the two species growing together.

As expected, when growing alone, both species of yeast followed the logistic curve, first growing fast and then slowing down until they saturated. The decline in growth occurred even before all sugar in the medium was consumed, because the accumulation of their waste product—ethanol—killed the young yeast buds. The kefir yeast grew much more slowly, and its saturating population alone totaled less than half that of the beer yeast alone. But the combined amount of yeast in the microcosms containing both species was lower than that of the beer yeast growing alone. What happened?

When growing together, the amount of yeast of each species was lower than the saturating population each would have reached in isolation. Further, the amount of ethanol produced was larger when two species were growing together than when either grew in isolation. Therefore, Gause concluded, the amount of ethanol attained toxic levels earlier in the mixed treatment than it would have from single species.

Gause repeated the experiment, now adding oxygen to the mix by aerating the microcosms in the same way you might aerate a home aquarium. The main results were the same: The saturation population was lower for each yeast species when growing together, even though the kefir yeast grew much faster than without oxygen, and its saturating population more than doubled. What Gause called "the coefficients of the struggle for existence" were predictable under defined environmental conditions, no matter how fast the species grew. That meant that, as he put it, "if we know the properties of two species growing separately . . . we can calculate theoretically the growth of species and their maximal volumes in a mixed population." In the case of yeast, the result of the competition between two species was determined by the accumulation of their waste product.

But that finding was still not enough for the brilliant young Soviet scientist.

In a methodic buildup of his analysis of species interactions, Gause then repeated the experiments, using another same-species pair, in this case his old experimental subject, *Paramecium caudatum,* and a similar species, *Paramecium aurelia.* But he added a twist: Now he would keep adding water and food to the microcosm daily, in an attempt to mirror the natural conditions where the energy from the sun is available daily without interruption—as opposed to previous experiments where food was limited and, once it was consumed, there was food no more. Gause's key question now was, "Will one species in these conditions drive the other one out completely, or will a certain equilibrium become established between them?"

Both species grew well separately and attained their saturating population in about 10 days, but the news here was that *P. aurelia* drove *P. caudatum* extinct in about two weeks when growing together—that is, when competing for the same food. Surprisingly, *P. caudatum* started to grow faster than *P. aurelia*, but *P. aurelia* was more resistant to waste products, making it competitively superior in the longer term.

This seminal finding was later named the "competitive exclusion principle," whereby two species that compete for the same resource cannot coexist at constant abundances. When one species has an advantage over the other, even the slightest one, it will dominate in the long term. The comparisons with our own interaction with the rest of species on Earth could not be more chilling.

THE NEXT STEP in Gause's work was to introduce one more level in the food web: a predator. With unplanned prescience, he named that chapter in his book "The Destruction of One Species by Another." The new extended ecosystem was now composed of three levels: bacteria → *Paramecium caudatum* → *Didinium nasutum*. *Didinium* is a barrel-shaped, single-cell organism that eats mostly *Paramecium*, even though *Didinium* is only half the length of *Paramecium*.

Volterra's mathematical equations (developed independently by his contemporary Alfred Lotka, an American scientist) suggested that in nature, a predator will never drive its prey extinct. This is what biologists believed all along: When the prey abundance decreases because of predation, it will be followed by a decline in predator abundance because of a shortage of food. But when the predators decline, the prey will increase again because of decreased predation, and so on. The Lotka-Volterra theory predicted periodic oscillations in the abundance of predators and prey, and field data supported the theory.

Once again, Gause was in for a surprise. He placed five individuals of *Paramecium* in his microcosms, and two days later added three predator *Didinium*. In his own words: "After the predators are put with the Paramecia, the number of the latter begins to decrease, the predators multiply intensely, devouring all the Paramecia, and thereupon perish themselves." In other words, the predators eat all the prey and subsequently become extinct because of the absence of food. Gause repeated the experiment many times, in vessels of different size, and adding the predators at different times, but the result was always the same: In the end, the predators could not help themselves, and everybody died.

This is not what we observe in the natural world, however, where predators and prey coexist in many different environments. A wonderful example comes from pure observation of an unintended experiment. Records of pelt trading by the Hudson Bay Company in Canada from the mid-1800s up to Gause's days showed an oscillation between the number of lynx (predator) and hare (prey) fur caught by trappers. The numbers of animals caught back then were small relative to the total size of the wild population, so trapping was probably not the main factor in explaining changes in lynx and hare numbers.

THE NATURE OF NATURE

The assumption was that the success of trapping lynx and hare reflected their abundances in the wild. There were cycles where lynx numbers increased and hare numbers decreased, followed by a decline in lynx numbers and an increase in hare numbers, and so on and so forth. Yet lynx never drove hares extinct. In the same way, lions in the African plains, wolves in temperate forests, or sharks in coral reefs never drive their prey extinct. So what happened differently in Gause's experimental microcosms?

Gause continued by replicating some natural conditions, adding variety in his little microcosms. His test tubes represented a homogeneous ecosystem, which does not exist in the real world. So he added sediment to the test tubes, where *Paramecium* could hide. As expected, *Didinium* ate all *Paramecium* outside of the sediment, while some *Paramecium* were able to escape by taking refuge within the sediment. *Didinium* does not hunt actively for prey—it only ingests whatever comes near it—so the prey in the sediment were safe. But that meant that soon there was no food available for *Didinium,* so the predator went extinct. Without the predator, *Paramecium* resumed growing until it reached its saturating population. Once again, it became hard for Gause to re-create the natural conditions of even the simplest food chain. Spatial refuges prevented the extinction of the prey but resulted in the extinction of the predator, while Lotka-Volterra equations predicted the oscillations in predator-prey numbers. What was missing here?

Gause then added another factor: immigration. He introduced a few *Didinium* predators every three days, and finally was able to re-create the lynx-hare oscillations observed in Canada and predicted by the mathematical models. The coexistence of predator and prey was possible if there were refuges for the prey and if the predator was not confined to a narrow space—a situation that is closer to what we can observe in the natural world.

Gause showed that two species can coexist even when they compete for the same resources, only at different abundances than when living without their competitors, and that the species that has an advantage over the use of resources in their environment is poised to be "dominant"—that is, more abundant than the other. Gause also showed that both a predator and a prey can coexist within the same environment, as long as the prey has some refuges to escape from the predator.

Our planet is home to millions of species, and ecosystems such as coral reefs and tropical forests harbor tens of thousands of species each, living together in what appears to be a miraculous balance. How do we move from two species to tens of thousands? How do species come together and create these magnificent ecosystems? It would take scientists studying natural environments over time and space to start to tackle these questions.

CHAPTER FOUR

SUCCESSION

IN 1970, two marine biologists based in Hawaii, Richard Grigg and James Maragos, wanted to understand how coral reefs develop over time. The longevity of some coral species—some live decades, if not centuries—made it impractical, however, for scientists to study them within their lifetimes. But Grigg and Maragos had an idea.

The island of Hawaii is crowned by the Kilauea volcano, which is still active and produces lava flows periodically. You might have seen footage of the lava flows reaching the ocean, either as a glowing red waterfall or as a crawling blob with the viscosity of tar. When the hot lava meets the Pacific Ocean, it crackles and hisses, boiling the seawater and creating violent explosions of white steam. The largest lava flows continue their path underwater, succumbing to gravity and hugging the bottom until they solidify and become part of the seafloor.

Lava is a destroyer of ecosystems. As lava flows smoothly over the slopes of a volcano, it vaporizes everything in its path and then buries it under a sarcophagus of basalt that hardens once the lava cools down—both above and under the water. At the same time, lava flows are regenerators of life, for by obliterating ecosystems, they provide a virgin substrate for species to colonize.

Grigg and Maragos discovered that accurate dates of lava flows had been recorded since 1801. They measured the diversity and abundance of different types of corals on underwater areas that had been covered by lava flows between 102 years and 1.6 years before their study. The ages of the different lava flows allowed them to substitute space for time in this natural experiment. They did not have to run an experiment for decades. The volcano had already done that for them.

Grigg and Maragos found that not all species of corals arrive at the same time. Some are "pioneers" that settle and grow fast, while others take longer to colonize. In exposed shallow areas, recovery time was 20 years, but in sheltered areas, it might take more than 50 years for the complete recovery of the coral reef.

Their study has several lessons for us. First, the pioneers that arrive first and grow fast might not be those that last long. The pioneers would be like the weeds that grow after a forest has been burned, with the trees taking longer to colonize.

Second, an ecological community in an environment that is more stable over time—a deeper reef, where wave action is less noticeable, for example—will require a longer time to form. That is because deep corals take a longer time to grow. Only a stable environment without major disturbances would allow for old coral colonies to develop. And they can be very old: A recent study showed that some deep coral communities in Hawaii are 15,000 years old. In shallow waters, in contrast, coral reefs are subject to the destructive force of tropical storms, so the only species able to colonize are the pioneers that grow fast.

Finally, the factors that go into forming an ecosystem are many. The lava flow study showed us that species with different traits—growth rates, for example—thrive at different times and places. Gause showed us that even a simple ecosystem with just three species—a prey, a predator, and a top predator—can be complex, and the relationships between species may change depending on changes in the environment. Then how can thousands of species come together and form mature, functioning ecosystems such as tropical forests and coral reefs? How do ecosystems develop? Are there ecosystem assembly rules, like do-it-yourself furniture instructions?

Let's think of a house. Nothing can be built until the foundations have been established. Only then we can start building the walls. The plumbing and the electrical system come only after the walls have been built. So do the doors and the roof. Masonry comes after the pipes have been installed. And the furniture should come only after all the hardware is in place. In summary, the assembly of a house has to follow a logical succession of steps. Does a forest, or a coral reef, get assembled the same way, following some type of ecological progression?

Even though species may not have an architectural plan, it turns out that ecosystems do assemble along a process that scientists call "ecological succession." Succession is driven by a small number of rules regarding how species arrive and in what sequence as they colonize a place—just as the different species of corals did on Hawaii's lava flows—and the properties emerging from that self-assembly.

IF ECOSYSTEMS in environments exposed to continuous disturbance cannot develop beyond some simple stages, what happens in an environment that is relatively stable for centuries, or millennia? Let's take a look at forests.

Forests are the most complex ecosystems on the land and contain over half of the different types of plants and animals. What is the ecological succession that leads to a mature forest? How does a forest start?

Picture the ancient forests of Earth, the so-called primary forests that have never been cut. A forest in the California Sierras, with sequoias as tall as a football field is long, which were already alive when the last great pyramid of Egypt was built. A forest in the eastern part of Poland, with oaks that sprouted from acorns when Columbus reached the Caribbean and are now more than 10 stories tall. The

Amazonian forest, with more different species growing on a single Brazil nut tree than all the species than can be found in a hectare of European soil. These forests are at least as old as the oldest tree in them. How did they assemble?

Let's now picture a fire that burns part of the forest to the ground. Where there was a green canopy, now there is black, scorched earth. Soon, however, new life emerges. If you are a European wild mushroom aficionado, you must know that morels and asparagus grow well in burned areas. My dad used to take me foraging when I was a child, when I developed a craving for sautéed mushrooms collected only hours before in pine and oak forests near home (which came in very handy for our nondiving days in Corsica years later). Even if you are not such an aficionado, you still might have seen green grass growing within weeks in an area that was burned. Where do these fungi and weeds come from?

Forest fires commonly only burn the upper part of the ground, leaving the soil underneath the surface intact. Within that soil are seeds of plants that have been waiting for their chance to have their day in the sun, literally. There is not much light under a thick forest canopy, so most plants cannot flourish. But their seeds can survive underground for decades. As an example, in some parts of the Atacama Desert in Chile, it never rains—never, at least, within a human lifetime. Thus the desert is an arid terrain with no conspicuous life. But in 2018 it rained in an area that had not had any rain for a hundred years. A few days later, what had been a barren yellow surface was now a multicolor carpet of wildflowers. These flowers in turn reproduced and produced seeds that ended up on the desert floor, and then they dried up after the miraculous effect of the rain had disappeared. Covered by dust and sand, those new seeds will also wait for their opportunity—their 15 days of fame. Maybe it will take another century. Nature does not rush, but she always gets things done.

Fungi do not produce seeds. They mostly spread through filaments that form massive webs in the soil upon which forests grow. The mushrooms that we all know, with their little hats, are reproductive parts that produce spores that the wind will disperse, spreading the fungus farther. Some fungi are parasites, but others are the glue that binds the soil and the forest together. Many plants, including trees, can only absorb nutrients from the soil thanks to a symbiosis with fungal filaments. Thus, the soil is like the foundation of the house. Without a foundation, there is no house. Without a living soil, with fungi, worms, insects, and microbes, there is no forest.

The weeds will grow using nutrients contained both in the soil and in the ashes of the former forest. By developing shallow roots and spreading, they will stabilize the burned ground and enable the seeds of other plant species, carried to the site by the wind, to germinate and grow. The weeds will attract insects, which will eat their leaves and blades. The insects will attract small birds that will eat them. Then a bird will fly over the patch and drop feces containing the seeds of a bush from elsewhere, which will grow, providing more habitat for other species. These pioneer species facilitate the arrival of others. They provide the enabling conditions for an ecosystem to develop.

Seeds of the dominant trees will eventually make it into the patch from surrounding unburned forests. Not all of them will survive to grow into trees. They will take a longer time, but in the end they will dominate the ecosystem, which now looks like a forest again. In due time, the canopy will be thick again and shade the ground below, thus relegating smaller plants that need abundant light to be patient and wait for another opportunity. Maybe lightning will burn a tree, which will fall and create an opening in the forest. Time for the pioneers again.

IN THE 1950S AND 1960S, Eugene Odum, an American ecologist, and a formidable Catalan ecologist, Ramón Margalef, among others, started to extract patterns from studies in different ecosystems and parts of the world. I have to admit a soft spot for Margalef because I was trained in his school of thought at the University of Barcelona and had the privilege of attending some of his lectures in his late university years. These giants of ecology had an extraordinary ability to identify patterns within masses of information and create wonderful syntheses.

Odum and Margalef realized that ecological succession was a sequence of processes that could be predicted. For instance, over time, a forest will be a puzzle of shrubs, small trees, and large trees of many species. Their abundance and their distribution will depend on many factors, such as whether birds or mammals have spread their seeds, or the slope of the terrain, or the acidity of the soil. Although we cannot predict what exact path ecological succession will take, we do know that grasses will colonize first, followed by shrubs, followed by trees. Some species will need the previous work, so to speak, done by other species to facilitate their arrival. For example, bromeliads are plants of astounding variety, with needle-thin to broad and flat leaves, soft or spiky, green, gold, or brown. Some of them, such as Spanish moss, live on top of other plants, typically trees—they are called epiphytes, a word derived from the Greek meaning "over plants." Tropical bromeliads can grow large and heavy; thus, they need sturdy branches of trees to grow on, and these trees in turn need fungi to provide an underground network that helps them absorb nutrients from the soil. It's facilitation upon facilitation.

What Odum and Margalef realized independently was that some properties emerge along ecological succession, regardless of the type of ecosystem. Some things happen over time that are predictable for coral reefs, wetlands, forests, grasslands, or your garden—if left unattended.

From a plethora of studies, they showed that over time, as the ecosystem matures, the number of species in a given area increases. This is because the abundance of the species that provide the living architecture of the ecosystem (plants in a forest, corals in a reef) also increases, and at the same time there is an increase in the three-dimensional complexity of the ecosystem. Not only the types of creatures increase; their total biomass—their weight—increases over time until it saturates, like the microbes growing in Gause's test tubes. At one point, the laws of physics do not allow larger trees or more leaves per square meter.

The more holes and nooks and cracks and crevices and tall trees and bushes and dead tree trunks, the more micro-habitats exist for different species to colonize. For example, some fungi only grow on dead tree trunks. Some species of fungi extremely rare in the United Kingdom were miraculously rediscovered only after the owners of a private estate let old dead trees follow their natural succession and decompose by natural forces. In the rest of the country, where dead trees are cut up and hauled away for firewood or mulch, those fungi are nowhere to be seen. Dead and dying trees are also preferred by many woodpeckers for nesting, because their wood is softer. In lowland tropical forests, a quarter of all plant species are likely to be epiphytes, like the orchids. Orchids not only show preferences for the species of tree they grow on, but also prefer to grow high on the canopy of tall trees—far from the shadow created by the tree's branches, where, incidentally, some shade-tolerant orchids can actually live. And so on ad infinitum.

The pioneers tend to be generalists—that is, species that can eat and grow whatever and wherever. As ecological succession progresses, the specialists arrive—that is, species that have more narrow requirements for survival, such as the species of hummingbird that only feeds on nectar from the flowers of a single type of tropical plant. Ecosystems advance toward a complexity that Margalef called the "baroque" of nature.

And the work provided by different species—the natural processes they perform—also changes over time. As a forest grows, its amount of wood and leaves increases over time. The productivity of the forest increases until it reaches a limit, and then it saturates. A forest will reach that limit when physically there is no room for more wood. At that point, the trees have created a canopy such that all the sunlight that can be used by the plants in the forest is being used. The trees will have reached such ages and sizes that it is physically impossible for them to grow larger.

During early successional stages, the weeds grow fast: In a week, they can double their biomass—a measure of their abundance in weight, for example, pounds per square meter. But a mature forest dominated by old trees will appear unchanging to human eyes. In other words, the more mature an ecosystem is, the more inhabitants it has, the more connections between them there are, and the slower it changes— the slower its turnover rate.

The growth of a forest is pure magic, a natural alchemy that we take for granted but that is unbelievable when one thinks about it—and an ongoing process that is helping us to avert climate catastrophe around the world. This is the where the magic lies: Plants use sunlight to turn an invisible gas in the air into growth. The invisible gas is carbon dioxide (CO_2), which is found naturally in Earth's atmosphere. Plants use the energy contained in sunlight to break the CO_2 into its constituent parts: carbon (C) and oxygen (O). They use the carbon to make sugars and grow, with the help of water, which brings essential nutrients such as nitrogen and phosphorus from the soil via the roots. They release the oxygen back into the atmosphere. The process of taking carbon out of the air and turning it into plant stuff—leaves, wood, or roots—is called carbon sequestration. The plants on Earth (from the microscopic algae in the open ocean to the giant sequoias in the American West) remove about half of our carbon pollution every year. As the forest matures along ecological succession, it stores more and more carbon—in wood but also in the soil. More magic tricks.

The more leaves are produced, the more dead leaves on the forest floor; that's nature's waste. But if the forest floor is its landfill, why don't we find a carpet of dead leaves several meters deep on the ground under a deciduous forest, like our own trash that we see accumulating everywhere? Because leaves are truly organic, biodegradable, and fully recyclable: They are the quintessential compost. In an older forest, there are plenty of insects, fungi, and bacteria that will eat and decompose the dead leaves into basic nutrients, which in turn will be reincorporated into the forest's food web, moving into the trees' roots with water. The natural world is a true circular economy, where there is no waste, but everything is reused to produce something else. Ironically, the more mature the ecosystem, the more detritus (waste) it produces, but the more important detritus is for regenerating nutrients, which keep the forest thriving.

There is more. We all have heard that the forests are the lungs of our planet, but actually most of the oxygen in the atmosphere has been produced by bacteria and microscopic algae in the ocean. In fact, much of the oxygen produced in a forest could be respired (literally, burned up for use as energy) by the activity of all the animals that live within, which use that oxygen to process the consumption of all the plant material produced by the forest. Instead, forests are the sweat glands of the planet. Trees pull water from the soil, move it up to their branches, and release it mostly as water vapor through their leaves. This process, equivalent to our own sweating, is called evapotranspiration—evaporation of water makes plants move water from the soil to their leaves, which will transpire, or give off that water as vapor into the surrounding air. The evaporation of our sweating cools our bodies down; evapotranspiration cools entire forests down.

At the end point of succession, the ecosystem reaches what is called its "climax"—the culmination of the growth process, where the ecosystem is at its most baroque and yet most efficient. But just how long do a particular ecosystem and its climax last?

Succession

MY FRIEND AND COLLEAGUE John Pandolfi is a pale-ontologist: He studies fossils to understand how life on Earth has evolved in the recent geologic past. John has studied Caribbean coral reefs in ancient terraces that emerged after the last glacial era, going back 115,000 years. He found that two species of fast-growing corals of the *Acropora* type dominate the fossil record on shallow reefs: the staghorn coral, with cylindrical branches that branch like the antlers of a deer, and the elkhorn coral, with fat, flat branches resembling the antlers of a moose. (Maybe it should be renamed "moose coral.") These are pioneers, weedy corals that grow fast. All Caribbean reefs get hammered by hurricanes every decade or so, their shallow corals broken every single time, but they manage to come back because the *Acropora* are able to grow fast and recolonize the reefs in between hurricanes.

Because damaging hurricanes and wave action are relatively frequent, the ecological succession of a typical shallow coral reef has never advanced beyond communities composed almost exclusively of elkhorn coral (shallower) and staghorn coral (just a little deeper). The cycle has been hurricane, coral rubble, *Acropora* reef, hurricane, rubble, *Acropora* reef, and so on and so forth—at least until the second half of the 20th century, when a combination of human activities changed the environment to such an extent that *Acropora* corals began to have a hard time surviving.

It takes a long time—centuries or millennia—for old ecosystems to assemble. Information takes a long time—and a long succession of events—to accumulate. But losing it all tends to happen catastrophically. A fire will destroy thousands of years of forest growth; a lava flow will destroy a centuries-old coral reef; building a shrimp farm can mean cutting down a centuries-old mangrove forest in days.

Natural disturbances like forest fires, lightning, or lava flows will reset the successional clock in parts of the ecosystems. It's the lightning that fells a large tree, opening a hole in a tropical forest canopy, or large herbivores rummaging about the temperate forest floor that will allow for succession to restart. Thus, an old forest won't necessarily be a full canopy of ancient trees, but a mosaic of patches at different successional stages: here old canopy, a patch of forest at its climax, there a just opened clearing, a younger canopy in a clearing that opened up a few decades ago somewhere else, and so on. A healthy mature ecosystem is not like a picture of a single color, but a multicolor quilt that evolves and responds to changes in the environment, and to changes within itself.

Our built environment also follows successional principles. China can now produce a massive city relatively quickly, but in the past, cities grew organically. When the first Dutch settlers started building in Manhattan, there were wooden shacks, a few basic jobs, and few public services. It took more than 200 years to grow from a few hundred people to more than eight million people with thousands of different jobs (the city equivalent of the different species' roles in a nonhuman ecosystem), from garbage pickers and doctors to canine hairdressers, speaking hundreds of languages. Today, New York City conserves none of the original dwellings, but it exhibits an exuberant variety of brick, steel, and glass buildings, from one story to 541 meters (1,775 ft) high, from pre-20th century to under construction, with and without doorman, with and without elevators. The growth rate of New York City has also slowed down over time: The size of the initial settlement may have doubled within a year, but presently the annual changes in the city are minuscule relative to its size and complexity. Only patches where buildings are torn down allow for regrowth, like clearings in a forest.

Despite these similarities, there is an inherent tension between ecosystem development and human progress. Humans want quantity over quality, growth over develop-ment, production over protection—usually realized in the most inefficient of ways. Natural ecosystems self-organize with an increase of species richness, size and age of organ-isms, biomass, productivity, efficiency in the recycling of organic matter, three-dimensional structure created by living organisms, and stability, among many other properties. But humans latch on to one idea and blindly focus on it. We turn mature ecosystems into monocultures—cultures of single species—which are the simplest of ecosystems. With our blinders on, we prioritize just one species, selected to grow fast—like cornfields in Iowa or salmon farms in the Chilean fjords—and we focus all our efforts on it to the detriment of any surrounding species. Although these monocultures are intended to feed us, ironically, they are the closest thing to a barren landscape when it comes to ecosystem maturity—the anti-climax. Our built environments are misguided attempts at re-creating the assembly and the productivity of natural ecosystems, designed to satisfy our needs.

We are abruptly interrupting and most often reversing ecological succession across the biosphere, turning complex ecosystems into simple, homogenous systems with fast turnover rates: That is, we are accelerating and fragmenting the biosphere. Does that mean that we are isolating ourselves from nature? Or are we immersing ourselves into nature more deeply than she can handle? These are questions worth asking as we try to learn from the ways of nature, and a way to answer these questions is to look at the boundaries between ecosystems.

CHAPTER FIVE

BOUNDARIES

O NCE A YEAR, a miracle occurs off the coast of South Africa. A seasonal wind running parallel to the coast displaces surface water alongside the shore. The water that moves away is replaced by water coming from the deep. The upwelling of deep water rich in nutrients creates a bloom of microscopic algae—phytoplankton—that thrives as it exploits the fertilizer brought up from the deep and the abundant sunlight. These algae blooms can be seen from space: beautiful green patches and eddies, visible in satellite photos.

As deep, nutrient-rich waters make it to the surface, they jump-start a planktonic succession, in the same way that a fallen tree restarts the forest succession. First, very small bacteria that conduct photosynthesis and small phytoplankton develop. They are followed by larger phytoplankton such as diatoms, which create glass skeletons using silica dissolved in seawater. An abundance of prey will inevitably result in greater opportunities for predators. As these large phyto-plankton become abundant, small animal predators show up, in turn attracting large predators, building an extraordinary food web with four or five levels. The predators of phytoplank-ton are also microscopic, mostly shrimplike animals—zoo-plankton. As the biomass of zooplankton develops, billions of sardines—predators of zooplankton—show up for their annual feast. Sometimes the sardine runs along the South African coast measure up to eight kilometers (5 mi) long.

And then, in a matter of just weeks, one of the most extraordinary food webs in the world assembles. The colos-sal abundance of sardines attracts large predators: tuna, sharks, seabirds, sea lions, dolphins, and large whales. Per-haps you have seen this feeding frenzy in nature documen-taries. A large school of sardines is surrounded by predators. As a defense mechanism, the sardine school packs itself into a tight ball—fatalistically called a bait ball—and starts spin-ning madly. The fast-moving ball of sardines makes it very difficult for a predator to chase a single individual. For the sardine, there is safety in numbers. But for the predators, there is efficiency in numbers. Tuna and dolphins push the bait ball closer to the surface, reducing the ability of the sardines to escape them. But danger also comes from the sky. Hundreds of birds such as boobies dive into the sea, capturing sardines one by one. Attacked from all angles, the sardine school is helpless, its volume reduced quickly. A final nail in the sardines' coffin may come from whales, taking advantage of the packing of the prey by other predators. In a single swoop, a large whale coming from the deep with mouth agape can ingest tens of thousands of sardines. In the end, all that's left of the sardines is a rain of shiny scales that sink to the seafloor.

What ecological principles can we extract from this wondrous spectacle? And what does this have to do with our exploitation of natural ecosystems?

The boundary between the plankton bloom—and later between the massive sardine run—and surrounding waters is sharp and asymmetrical: Here is a thick soup of plankton and sardines, and a few feet away there is just water. But that boundary is permeable and active because predators come in and out of it. Energy—in the shape of food that organisms need to survive—also moves across the boundary.

Inside the plankton bloom, on one side of the boundary, we can find an ecosystem in early stages of succession: fast-growing microscopic algae, with a fast turnover rate. The productivity of these plankton blooms is astounding, with individual phytoplankton dividing at least once a day. The ecosystem at the other side of the boundary is home to large vertebrates, whose turnover rate is much lower—it takes many decades to double the size of a population of whales, for example.

The energy produced in the least mature ecosystem—food in the shape of phytoplankton, and later zooplankton—will cross the boundary and move to the more mature ecosystem surrounding it—the open waters that are home to marine mammals and the coastal zone that harbors seabirds.

In this way, the mature ecosystem exploits the less mature. The movement of energy moves only in that direction, although the capacity to control moves in the opposite direction. In the South African example, the productivity of the phytoplankton is exported to predators living around it, but the predators determine the lifetime of the sardine run. Large predators regulate the abundance of prey and thereby the structure of the ecological community.

This is a general pattern found in most asymmetrical boundaries in nature: Across an active boundary, the energy produced in the least mature side is used to allow the more mature side to move along its ecological succession. This is a pattern that occurs in space as much as in time. For instance, forest animals like deer shelter in the forest but move to clearings or nearby meadows to graze. The deer eat the meadow plants before they can grow much, hence grazing keeps the meadows in immature stages of the ecological succession. The energy produced by the grasses in the meadows cannot be used for the meadow community to advance along succession, but that energy is exported—via deer feces—to the forest, and there it serves as fertilizer and helps maintain the forest's mature state. The meadow produces new grass biomass equivalent to several times its standing biomass and respires (or burns energy) much less than the energy it produces. In contrast, a mature forest may respire all of its production and thus yield no excess productivity. In this case, the forest exploits the meadow.

ECOLOGICAL SUCCESSION within a single community is based on the same trend: Energy produced in one successional stage is used within the ecosystem to increase the maturity of the entire system. But sometimes a community does not become more mature. When that happens, there can be two main explanations.

First, as we saw in the coral reef environment in Hawaii, continuous high-energy physical disturbance puts a limit on how far a community can advance along its ecological succession. There, the high wave energy in shallow reefs does not allow for the formation of large coral colonies with complex structures. Second, succession can be stopped in a given community because a more mature system is exploiting it. This is the case of the sardine run hunted by its predators. Without exploitation, that sharp boundary between the plankton bloom and the surrounding water would take a longer time to disappear. Similarly, in the case of the deer grazing in the meadows, the boundary between the forest and a clearing will persist only if the more stable ecosystem, the forest, exploits the clearing.

Do all boundaries occur between two contiguous ecosystems? Not necessarily: Some boundaries can occur between ecosystems that are located far from each other. When I worked at the Scripps Institution of Oceanography in California, I always had binoculars on my desk, ready for looking for gray whales, which migrate twice a year between Alaska and Baja California, Mexico, swimming north during the summer months to feed in the rich waters of Alaska. Humpback whales conduct similar migrations in the Southern Hemisphere, swimming between the tropical eastern Pacific waters off Colombia and the Chilean fjords.

The gray whales migrate toward the increased daylight in the Alaska summer, which creates plankton blooms that in turn sustain an explosion of invertebrates and coastal fish. Summer is the season with the higher turnover rate, where more food is produced than can be consumed by predators. The whales use that window of opportunity, traveling north as food becomes more abundant and preparing themselves for the reproductive season. In the fall, they swim in the opposite direction, toward the shallow coastal lagoons of Baja California where, sheltered from the weather, they will give birth and mate. Once the baby whales are ready, the gray whales will conduct their northward migration and swim to Alaska once again. In this example, animals on the move create an active boundary between two ecosystems located 3,700 kilometers (2,300 mi) apart.

Birds conduct seasonal migrations and moving active boundaries of even greater magnitude. A small seabird, the sooty shearwater, migrates between the Bering Sea and Antarctic waters every year. It makes a journey across the entire Pacific Ocean in a figure eight pattern, traveling 64,000 kilometers (39,770 mi) in a year. The 114-gram (4 oz) arctic tern flies more than 70,000 kilometers (43,500 mi) between Greenland and Antarctica each year. These birds would be the envy of frequent fliers.

Many species of birds that nest in the northern European summer, when insects are bountiful, migrate to Africa in the winter. One of my favorites is the Eleonora's falcon, which nests on vertical limestone cliffs of some Mediterranean islands. This falcon raises its chicks later than any other falcon in the Mediterranean, its nesting season timed with the southward migration of the European swallow. No need to say what the falcons feed their chicks. This is another example of how migratory animals exploit different ecosystems during different seasons, and thus create active boundaries as they travel.

Not all boundaries in nature are asymmetrical. From a distance that allows us to see the entire mountain, the border between an oak forest and a pine forest in Corsica looks like a distinct line. But if we walk up that mountain and climb the transition between them, the line becomes fuzzy: First, we will observe a forest dominated by oaks; a little higher, the first pines will appear among the oaks; eventually, the oaks will become less abundant, until we see the last oak within a forest dominated by pines. This type of border can be considered symmetrical, because if we drew a line between the two forests, on each side we would see a mixed transition forest, with similar numbers of oaks and pines. There are symmetrical borders in the built environment as well: the transition between a city's suburbs—looking like an octopus extending its tentacles out from the city center—and the natural environment around, for example.

BOUNDARIES BETWEEN NATURAL SYSTEMS can be symmetrical—with smooth changes from one ecological community to another—or asymmetrical—when the change between communities is sharp. Asymmetrical boundaries can be maintained by physical barriers—such as the banks of a river—or because the ecosystem on one side of the boundary exploits the other one. The exploiter tends to be the more mature ecosystem, and there is a net flow of energy from exploited to exploiter. What does this mean for human ecosystems and our interaction with the rest of the biosphere?

Humans extract energy—in the shape of wood, fossil fuels, or living organisms—from natural ecosystems, and by doing so, they reverse ecological succession within those ecosystems. Like the whales eating the sardines, humans prevent natural ecosystems from becoming more mature and advancing along ecological succession. We are the ultimate exploiters of nature. The energy we extract from the natural world around us flows in one direction: toward us and our built environment.

In doing so, we create asymmetrical boundaries, both within natural ecosystems and between natural and human ecosystems. A boundary within a natural ecosystem would be the edge between a forest and a clearing cut by loggers. A boundary between a natural ecosystem and a human ecosystem would be the edge of the salt marsh near JFK airport in New York. These are all asymmetrical boundaries, and quite active, for we keep exploiting these ecosystems in what has become a chronic exploitation of the natural world.

Like the birds migrating across the planet—using energy from the north to reproduce in the south—humans create asymmetrical boundaries throughout the planet. Think, for example, of a rich tropical forest in Borneo, a mature ecosystem supporting one of the highest diversity of species in the world. Humans clear-cut it and replace it with an oil palm plantation, a monoculture with near-zero diversity. Only a scorched forest would be less ecologically mature than a plantation. The palm oil will be consumed in food products in cities around the world, but humans will not return anything to that ecosystem in exchange. As long as humans maintain the plantation, that habitat will never see a return to its former ecological glory, and the asymmetrical boundary between the forest and the plantation will persist.

DO THESE ECOLOGICAL PRINCIPLES—creation and maintenance of boundaries where one side exploits the other—also apply to the interaction *among* humans? Are there boundaries between cultures, nations, civilizations, or even neighborhoods with the same characteristics as those in nature? If so, what can we learn from nature that can help us solve some of our most challenging societal issues?

The border between Tijuana and San Diego is asymmetrical and sharp, for example, as is the entire border between the United States and Mexico: one country on one side of the line, the other on the other. All over the world, asymmetrical boundaries exist between political entities, but today's active borders need not happen in physical proximity. Global travel, shipping, and trade have created many more active boundaries.

In the natural world, the more mature ecosystem exploits the less mature with which it shares a boundary, thus preventing the latter from advancing along its successional trajectory. This suggests that an exploitative nation state can prevent the further development of another nation.

The gross domestic product (GDP) is the golden idol that most governments use to measure development. GDP, the monetary value of all finished goods and services made within a country during a year, is used to estimate an economy's size and rate of growth—but it's one of the worst indicators for human prosperity. First, it does not factor into its calculus the destruction of the natural world and, indeed, externalizes such devastating consequences in favor of manufacturing capabilities. For instance, if a flood destroys a town, reconstruction activities will make GDP grow—even though the flood itself could have been prevented with healthier ecosystems, which retain rainwater. Second, it assumes that the only value of a society is what can be measured as part of an official, organized market. Forest protection by an indigenous tribe would not be included in the GDP—but clear-cutting the forest for timber to be sold to another country would. Third, it does not measure well-being and happiness. "Less developed" countries are being asked to cut down their forests to grow crops for industrialized countries. Much of that energy is not being put to use in the ecosystem that is producing it—but instead it is being used to support and even boost richer countries. It is a situation like predators exploiting the plankton bloom or deer grazing at the forest's edge. It prevents "less developed" countries from maintaining cultural maturity, even fostering cultural regression.

It is important to acknowledge that every human society realizes its own cultural and ecological succession. There is no single climax for human societies, but many—just as not every ecosystem on land would develop into a forest. Not every nation needs to build New York City or Dubai. My friend and fellow National Geographic Explorer-in-Residence Wade Davis put it beautifully: "Whether human raw genius and potential is exercised in stunning works of technological innovation, as has been the great historical achievement of the West, or through the untangling of the complex threads of memory inherent in a myth—a primary concern, for example, of the Aborigines of Australia—is simply a matter of choice and orientation, adaptive insights and cultural priorities."

Many indigenous groups live amid the natural environment in a mosaic of patches at different successional stages. Their life practices create symmetrical boundaries with much finer grain, which helps to preserve the natural diversity of the ecosystems they call home, such as the indigenous lands in the Brazilian Amazon that look so green in satellite photos alongside the brown rectangular patches clear-cut nearby for nonindigenous cattle and agriculture. The indigenous peoples' cultural choice is not "less developed," as many seem to believe. If the West had seen forests as sacred entities

instead of a commodity, we may be suffering fewer human—
and economic—consequences of global heating.

LET'S GO BACK to New York as an example of how boundaries create inequality in the human world. The boundary
between New York City and the farmland upstate is asymmetrical and active. Because New York is connected to more
than 100 countries worldwide via shipping and air traffic, it
has many more borders than just the physical one with
farmland to the north. We could say that New York City is a
mature urban ecosystem. Its human diversity is astounding,
with 800 different languages spoken, which is a good proxy
for the nationalities of people living in the city. The mass of
nonliving structures—in this case, concrete, metal, and
glass, the equivalent of wood in a forest—is massive. And
the turnover rate is relatively low: Although construction
sites are everywhere, the city does not experience significant
relative annual growth in infrastructure.

But I would argue that New York City is a hypermature
ecosystem, maintained artificially and only thanks to the
exploitation of many other ecosystems across its boundaries. For example, the city does not produce much food. If it
didn't bring food from agricultural areas in the United States
and beyond, there would be mass human die-off.

New York City does not produce much energy either; it
has to import most of it from power plants elsewhere in the

state. It does not have its own freshwater, drawing it instead from the Catskill Mountains north of the city. Same for most materials to maintain the city.

If an impermeable border surrounded New York City—a tall wall that isolated it from the rest of the world—the human population would dramatically crash inside the perimeter. It is the exploitation of other areas in the United States and other countries of the world that maintains the maturity of New York City. Extend this principle to the United States as a whole: It is the exploitation of the Midwest farmlands—occupying formerly rich and diverse tall-grass prairies with unique biodiversity—and of many other countries around the world that keeps the United States' urban centers in their hyperdeveloped state, where consumption far exceeds production and more resources are consumed than are truly needed. Sure, the United States pays for those resources in organized markets, and no country should expect to be self-sufficient in a globalized world, but the reality is that there is a net flow of energy from other countries to the United States. Today, China, moving along a Western-style successional trajectory, is also developing thanks to its exploitation of other countries.

As long as energy and resources flow from "poor" to "rich" countries, the former will not be able to invest that energy in moving along their own successional trajectories—whatever those societies want it to be. The boundaries between rich and poor countries will persist, and the asymmetry of those boundaries will perpetuate global inequality. The United Nations' goal of worldwide sustainable development may be an illusion as long as we maintain these asymmetrical bound-aries and the relationships of energy and productivity that they perpetuate, and as long as the powers that be insist that there is only one way to measure human progress.

Let's return to the question of whether GDP accurately measures the maturity of a human society. My proposal is that we could instead be assessing the level of our knowledge of the other species in their environment and the sustainable relationship that has been developed with them. This is information that the human population has accumulated over time, and it is information that can help us use our natural environment—rather than abuse it. Instead of GDP, let's measure EMI (Environmental Maturity Index). Many wealthy countries that boast of inflated GDPs would be sur-prised to find that they land at the bottom of the EMI list.

There are many ways to see the world. This is the view of an ecologist.

Recognizing asymmetrical boundaries is the key to under-standing how energy moves between ecosystems. It can also help us understand our abuse of natural ecosystems and the inequalities that exist between industrialized countries and other countries. But we don't we see that scale of abuse or inequality in nature. Why not? Aren't there top predators with the potential to transform ecosystems the way we do? Are there species with stronger impact than others, able to dom-inate across boundaries as we humans do?

CHAPTER SIX

ARE ALL SPECIES EQUAL?

OBERT T. PAINE was a giant, not only because he towered above six feet but also because he made such significant scientific contributions. After completing his postdoctoral research at the Scripps Institution of Oceanography, he took a faculty job at the University of Washington in Seattle. I met Bob shortly before I became a professor at Scripps myself, in 1999. He told me how a little experiment changed his life—and ecological science—forever.

Bob had been a student of Fred Smith at the University of Michigan. He remembered one class when Smith pointed to a tree on the university campus and asked his students why it was green. "Chlorophyll" was the easy answer: the pigment in leaves that helps extract energy from the sun. Yes, chlorophyll gives leaves their green color, but why are there even leaves on this tree? Why don't the caterpillars eat them all? They seem like such an abundant supply of food! Smith's more sophisticated answer to his question was that the world is green because herbivores don't consume all plant material, since predators keep the herbivores in check. That is, caterpillars are not as abundant as they could be because birds eat them. That idea later became known as the "green world hypothesis," and it made Bob think about the role of predators in shaping our environment.

In 1963, Bob was a new professor at the University of Washington, and he was looking for a place to study what predators do to the ecosystems they inhabit. He discovered the Pacific shore and its intertidal zone, the region that is bathed by the rising tide and then dries during the low tide. It represents a symmetrical boundary between sea and land. The marine creatures living there have an abundant supply of water rich in nutrients every six hours, but they also emerge and have to survive out of water for hours at a time. The boundary between the sea and the land comes and goes, rhythmically. Living at the edge of two worlds has its pros and cons.

Bob found that the intertidal zone of the Washington shore was rich and productive, with large abundances of algae and invertebrates, such as anemones, sea urchins, limpets, barnacles, mussels, sponges, and a distinctive sea star, *Pisaster ochraceus*. *P. ochraceus* is purple and orange, with five arms, thick and curved like a bodybuilder's. Bob called that ecological community his nirvana. Like a good naturalist, he spent countless hours in the field, acquainting himself with the species living there and observing who ate whom. He would turn sea stars and sea urchins over to see what was on their mouths, note what type of barnacle a snail was attacking, and watch mussels open their shells as the tide came in, loaded with plankton.

Bob focused on the food web at Makah Bay, a three-and-a-half-hour drive west of Seattle, where he found sea urchins and limpets eating algae, snails eating barnacles, and *P. ochraceus* at the top of the food web, eating mussels and almost every other invertebrate. He wondered what would happen if he removed the top predator. Bob looked at a sea star, and after some thinking, he picked it up and threw it to deeper water. That was the moment that would change Bob's life, experimental ecology, and my life as well.

Bob threw another sea star to deeper waters, and another, and so on. He depopulated a single outcrop of sea stars in a nondestructive way. (The sea stars survived in deeper waters.) But he also left other areas untouched, as controls. That's the way scientific experiments work: Manipulate the factors you want to understand in one treatment, maintain the same factors without change in another, and then compare the outcome. Medical researchers call this a randomized controlled trial, and it is a sine qua non of scientific research. If we manipulate something in nature and want to know what the effects are, we need to compare it with an unmanipulated control. We also need to conduct manipulations in several different areas, or experimental plots, alongside several control plots.

Bob would drive to his study site to hit the low summer tides, clean the outcrop of *P. ochraceus*, make measurements of the abundance of different species in the experimental plots and the control plots, and drive back home to Seattle. "After only a year and a half," he said, "I knew that I hit ecological gold." So what had happened?

When sea stars were removed, nobody was there to eat the mussels. Therefore, the mussels could expand, occupying more of the intertidal rock. But other species were living there and occupying that rock. Fortunately for the mussels, they had a competitive advantage (like the *Paramecium aurelia* in Gause's test tubes that dominated over *P. caudatum*): They could overtake other organisms. And so they did, overgrowing and smothering everything else. For creatures that live attached to the bottom of their environment and survive by filtering seawater, as mussels do, space is everything. And in the absence of predators, mussels gained the competitive advantage for space.

In only a year and a half after the removal of *Pisaster ochraceus*, the intertidal community went from 15 different species to eight. And in seven years, the whole intertidal zone turned into a monoculture: Mussels were the only species left, having pushed all other species out. Those results were surprising, though. You would expect that removing the top predator, the *P. ochraceus* sea star, would increase the abundance of everything else below them.

To ensure that *P. ochraceus* was indeed special, Bob removed other species from the community. But he found the effect of removing others very small. As George Orwell wrote in his book *Animal Farm*, "All animals are equal, but some animals are more equal than others." In ecological terms, that means that not all species have the same impact on the community they inhabit. Bob's simple experiment proved, for the first time, that a single species—*Pisaster ochraceus*—can determine the composition of an entire ecological community. Shortly after, Bob published one of the most important papers in ecological science, proposing the idea of a "keystone species" and showing that *P. ochraceus* is a keystone species in the intertidal ecosystem he had been studying.

In architecture, the keystone is the stone in the middle and at the top of an archway that keeps the arch together and standing: Remove it, and the whole structure collapses. Remove *P. ochraceus,* and the whole structure of the intertidal ecosystem goes away. Bob defined a keystone as a species that has an effect on the entire ecosystem, not just on the species that it eats. And the impact of a keystone species is disproportionately greater than its abundance. That is, a predator is a keystone species when its abundance is relatively low—but its per capita effect is going to be disproportionately high. Few but powerful. Remove that species, and the community changes dramatically, typically becoming much simpler, with less diversity.

Most known keystone species are top predators, but there are species that aren't at the top of the food chain that still have a tremendous influence on the ecosystem. What are they, and how can they help us understand how human activities are changing the natural world?

ANOTHER GIANT of American experimental marine ecology, Paul Dayton, did his doctoral work under Bob Paine's supervision, also studying the intertidal zone off the coast of Washington State. He found the time to start a scientific diving program in Antarctica, too, in heroic times where he and his buddies conducted an aggregate of 500 dives, wearing old wet suits in waters at minus 1.5°C (–29.3°F). Today we dive in those waters inside dry suits and wearing three layers of technical underwear!

Paul was based off McMurdo Station, one of the scientific bases run by the United States. There was concern that the permanent human presence, together with the pollution caused by activities on the land, ice, and sea there, would have a detrimental effect on the previously pristine ecosystem. A great naturalist and ecologist, he first tried to understand the organization of the ecological community in the bay. He quickly realized that studying the effect of pollution on each species in the community separately would take a long time and a great deal of funding. Measuring the effects of pollutants on the interactions of all the species in the community would be impractical, especially in an environment where divers cannot stay submerged for more than half an hour at a time, even when wearing a wet suit, because of the unforgiving pain caused by the frigid waters. He had to come up with a shortcut.

Thus Paul thought that he should identify the species that have a disproportionately important influence on the structure of the community. Once they were identified, it would be easier to consider the effects of the pollutants or other disturbances on them, and thus indirectly on the rest of the community. For these Paul introduced the definition of "foundation species," but he clearly distinguished foundation species from keystone species. What's the difference? One of the best examples came from Paul's later research.

After obtaining his Ph.D. at the University of Washington, Paul went to work at Scripps, where he started the longest running study on giant kelp forests. Giant kelp is the redwood of the sea, its long strands like pillars starting as deep as 120 feet and reaching all the way up to the surface, sometimes growing a foot and a half a day. Every kelp is anchored to the bottom by a cone-shaped mesh of holdfasts from which dozens of stems, called stipes, arise. Gas-filled bladders about the size of large olives dot the stipes, which are crowned by broad, leaflike blades. Giant kelp continues to grow even once it reaches the surface, creating a canopy atop the water's surface through which sunlight filters as if through the stained glass of a cathedral. I have to admit to having a soft spot for Paul and his kelp forests, because once I moved to Scripps, I conducted research on kelp under his supervision.

Giant kelps provide the architecture of an entire ecological community. Their intricate holdfasts are inhabited by hundreds of worms, crustaceans, sponges, and many other creatures. Their blades are covered by little tube-forming worms and other invertebrates. Just beneath the kelp forest is an understory of smaller kelps, together with fleshy and coralline red algae, amid which sea urchins, abalones, and snails make their living. Like birds in a terrestrial forest, fish inhabit the giant kelp forest at all levels, some specializing in eating shrimplike creatures living on the kelp stipes, some grazing the algae of the understory, and others—such as the imposing black sea bass—eating every other fish in the food web. The giant kelp is the foundation species for this entire community: It provides the conditions for the diversity and abundance of species. Remove the kelp, and most other species go away.

Therefore, foundation species provide the structural basis of the ecosystem—its physical habitat—whereas keystone species keep the ecosystem going. Keystone species can be few and powerful, with a large influence on their ecosystem, but foundation species tend to be numerous and omnipresent. Just a few *P. ochraceus* sea stars (keystone species) can regulate the structure of their intertidal community, but it takes many kelp plants (foundation species) to form a kelp forest with its full complement of species.

One might then ask: Can there be keystone and foundation species in the same ecosystem? How do they interact with each other, and what are the implications for the ecosystem?

Back in the 1960s, Bob Paine had observed that inter-tidal pools at Tatoosh Island in Washington State were full of sea urchins, which had eaten all of the kelp. Bob saw there a clear violation of Smith's green world hypothesis: Here was a place where herbivores did denude all their plant prey. So he did what had worked so well for him in the past: He removed all sea urchins from some pools and left others untouched. The results were almost immediate. In the pools without sea urchins, kelp started growing fast. But he still questioned why sea urchins were naturally so abundant there.

Another scientist, Jim Estes, would be touched by seren-dipity—and Bob's influence—and come up with the answer. Jim is another tall and impressive scientist, handsome and soft-spoken. He was studying sea otters in Alaska, furry marine creatures that are the epitome of cuteness. Jim had met Bob at a bar (this is not a joke) and had told him about his intention to conduct a study on the physiology of sea otters, considering how energy flows in the Alaska ecosystem, from the kelp all the way up the food web to sea otters and larger species such as orcas. Bob, after listening to Jim, told him he did not find that idea too interesting, and asked whether he had thought of understanding what otters do to the system instead. One could try that by replicating Bob's species removal experiment. But how do you remove sea otters from some kelp forests while keeping them in others?

A thriving sea otter fur trade had started in the mid-1700s in Alaska, and that had wiped out most of the otters from the region. But a few survived, and laws passed to protect sea otters in 1911 helped to replenish the species along the Alaska coast. Some islands, like Amchitka, which Jim knew well, had recovered their sea otters. At Amchitka, sea urchins were common but very small, and kelps were abundant.

But then Jim dived at Shemya Island, where otters had not come back for some reason. "The most dramatic moment of learning in my life happened in less than a second, and that was sticking my head in the water at Shemya Island," Jim said years later. "It was just green with urchins and no kelp." The underwater world of Shemya looked like Bob's pools in Tatoosh: The dominant herbivore—the sea urchin—had removed all its prey—the kelp. And without the kelp, all other species were gone as well, including the otter.

Sea otters love to eat sea urchins, and so Jim realized that the absence of otters had likely caused the explosion of urchins. He had found another keystone predator: In this community, it was the sea otter, at the top of a food chain formed by otters eating sea urchins eating kelp. Sea otter removal had caused indirect effects throughout the food web, from carnivores to herbivores to plants. Bob Paine had called those indirect effects in the food web "trophic cascades": situations where predators control the structure of the ecosystem from the top down.

Twenty years later, Jim was having a hard time finding otters in Alaska; they seemed to be declining, and he also had a hard time finding a plausible explanation. There was enough food, so starvation could not be a cause. And they did not show signs of disease. But a colleague of Jim's, Brian Hatfield, met him at Amchitka Island one evening and told him that he had seen an orca attack a group of otters. Jim was skeptical. Orcas—killer whales—are the most formidable predator in the ocean, eating everything that's large, including whales, Steller sea lions, and even the feared white shark. Large animals, especially those with a high concentration of fat in their tissues, are a preferred item in their diet. No way would they be eating candy when they could be eating steaks. But Hatfield saw another attack at precisely the same place the next day. The following winter Jim's technician, Tim Tinker, also saw orcas eating otters at Adak Island.

Clam Lagoon, Alaska, provided another extraordinary natural site for an experiment. The bay had a narrow entrance, narrow enough to allow sea otters to come in and out but too tight for orcas. Jim and his colleagues found abundant sea otters in the bay, even though in nearby areas, orcas were common. Jim had found another keystone predator, a longer trophic cascade, and an extraordinary story of indirect effects, but in this case, it would turn out to be humans who were at the top of the food web, causing unexpected changes across ecosystems and decades.

Alan Springer of the University of Alaska, Fairbanks, envisioned an intriguing hypothesis to explain the otter-orca phenomenon. After World War II, Japanese and Russian whalers started killing whales on an industrial scale. By the late 1960s, they had removed nine out of 10 whales in the North Pacific. (Orcas were too small to be of any harvest value, and thus their numbers were not directly diminished by industrial whaling.) A type of orca also specialized in killing large whales. The hunting of large whales offshore triggered a cascade of changes: Without large whales to prey on, those orcas had to move closer to shore and eat other species. Orcas first went after harbor seals—smaller than sea lions but fatter and more energy rich. When they had depleted the harbor seal population, they started eating sea lions, and when there were few sea lions left, sea otters. As the sea otters dwindled, their prey—the sea urchins—thrived, eating away the kelp and creating barrens, stripped of all the animals that a healthy kelp forest supports. As Jim said, "The amazing part of that was the notion that something like whaling that started in the middle of the 20th century, way out in the oceanic realm of the North Pacific, could affect something like urchins and kelp in the coastal ecosystem. It was mind-blowing . . . almost like science fiction."

WHEN I WAS AN UNDERGRADUATE at the University of Barcelona in the 1980s, I learned about Bob Paine's, Paul Dayton's, and Jim Estes' studies. The type of work they did appealed to me, combining time in the field, experimentation, and ecological theory. I was an avid diver who could not get enough time underwater. Most of my early diving, after I turned 18 and was legally allowed to scuba dive, took place in the Costa Brava in Catalonia. I was used to a sea with clear water, a few small fish, and an ocean floor turned into a barren because of the grazing activity of too many sea urchins—like at Shemya Island in Alaska. And then I did my first dive in the Medes Islands Marine Reserve, where fishing was prohibited, close to the border between France and Spain. There I saw what Jim saw in Shemya, but in reverse: Inside the reserve there were lots of large fish, sea urchins were rare, and little algal forests covered the bottom.

The subject of my Ph.D. thesis was settled: I would study the effects of removing predatory fish, using the marine reserve and the unprotected areas nearby as the site of my natural experiment, and I would conduct experimental removals to test the impact of the predators. I spent hundreds of hours underwater. I scraped samples of the miniature algal forest and the hundreds of little creatures within, later identifying and counting them under a microscope. I counted fish and sea urchins while diving. I observed what the fish ate and installed plastic cages underwater to control the predation factor so that fish could not access their prey. And I spent hours simply watching what was going on around me. After three years of fieldwork, my data revealed a story similar to that of my scientific heroes. Where fishing was prohibited, the fish were abundant and the ecological community was thriving. Everybody was there: big and small fish, algae, and all the smaller species that thrive in the same ecosystem—and even sea urchins, but not too many, and hiding. Where the fish had been removed by fishing, the sea urchins had proliferated, eating the algal forest away and leaving a barren seafloor. A trophic cascade in the Mediterranean.

I found that predators not only reduce the abundance but also change the behavior of their prey. The Mediterranean shallow rocky bottoms go through the seasons, just as the land does. In the winter, seawater temperatures drop to 12°C (53.5°F). Days are short and algal abundance is low, but as the days lengthen and seawater temperature increases through spring and summer, the ecosystem flourishes. Algae grow fast. Miniature forests expand to as much as a foot in height, sometimes containing more than 100 different types of algae in an area no larger than a dinner plate. During the warmer months, the boulders in the Medes Islands Marine Reserve wore a biological wig of sorts, a healthy tuft of brown and red algae that covered all but the bottom third of the boulder. It was as if a barber had shaved the base of the boulders. What was the reason for that pattern, I wondered?

Looking more closely, I saw sea urchins tucked inside the space between the boulders and the seafloor. Maybe they were responsible. During the day, with all the predatory fish swimming around, these sea urchins were hiding. What happened during the night, when most fish were resting? There was only one way of knowing. I returned at night and dived on the boulders. As predicted, the large fish were nowhere to be seen, but at the base of the boulders, sea urchins had now come out from under and were grazing on the algae growing nearby, creating halos that extended about a meter around each boulder. A meter: That's the distance a sea urchin was able to crawl at night before having to return to hide during daylight hours. Similar halos have been observed in other ecosystems, such as in Caribbean seagrass beds. There, sea urchins graze out circles around patch reefs where they shelter from predators during the day and conduct feeding excursions at night.

Everywhere we look, we find the same pattern: When the predators are there, their prey is less numerous and more scared. It's a landscape of fear, but the community is more diverse. Remove the top predators, and the ecosystem collapses.

Field biologists have found this in temperate forests, where the presence of wolves makes their deer prey spend less time eating in the open, thus fostering the growth of forests. In grasslands, grasshoppers are more wary and eat less grass in the presence of spiders, thereby enhancing grass growth. In pristine coral reefs such as Kingman Reef in the Line Islands, I have seen plenty of sharks swimming around but few of their prey, which I found to be hiding among the corals during the day. In lakes, predatory largemouth bass control the abundance of minnows that eat zooplankton; the minnows spend more time hiding from the bass, thus their zooplankton prey abounds, in turn controlling the abundance of phytoplankton—thus making lake waters crystal clear. Similar examples are found in ecosystems across our planet.

The conclusion is unavoidable: If we want a diverse and rich world, we need to keep the predators there. Keystone predators are particularly important, and most fragile. They are the fewest in number and yet the species with the strongest impact on their ecological communities. They also tend to be the first species that humans eliminate from an ecosystem when they show up: wolves, sharks, sea otters.

But not only the keystone species are important; so are the foundation species, which provide the architecture for the entire community. Often species sit in the middle of the food web, but their presence can also be critical. Take the example of the long-spine sea urchin *(Diadema antillarum)* in the Caribbean.

Decades of overfishing in the Caribbean meant fewer large fish, including the large parrotfish that eat algae and the triggerfish and porgies that eat adult *D. antillarum*. By the 1980s, *D. antillarum* were incredibly abundant, with average densities of 10 urchins per square meter in Jamaica. A voracious eater of algae, *D. antillarum* kept their growth in check, so the coral reef stayed healthy, dominated by corals.

But in 1983–84, *D. antillarum* suffered a mass die-off across the Caribbean, caused by an as yet unidentified disease. Hurricanes and increased nutrient runoff from agriculture fostered blooms of large brown algae amid the coral reefs. In decades past, parrotfish and surgeonfish would have controlled the algae. With them gone, *D. antillarum* was the last significant herbivore—a species that maintained a delicate balance within its ecosystem. After the sea urchin die-off, though, the large brown algae had no predators, hence they overgrew and smothered the coral, putting another nail in the coffin of Caribbean reefs.

THANKS TO THE WORK of passionate field ecologists like Bob Paine, Paul Dayton, and Jim Estes, we are beginning to understand the importance of a few large species in their roles as keystone or foundation species. Unfortunately, we don't know what most species do, though. It would be impractical to perform the thousands of experiments that would be required to determine the impact of every species in its community. But one thing we do know, as Bob said: "To ignore the fact that there are top-down effects is to invite mistakes."

One way to think of the role of species in their communities is to think of them as having ecological jobs. Using our analogy of the city, New York probably has thousands of different jobs, from mayor to pizzamaker to pet hairdresser. Each has a different role and impact within the community—the urban equivalent of species within their communities. Can we live without some species? Well, it depends on what their role is. To return to the city analogy: If all the canine stylists in New York City went away, some ladies on the Upper East Side would be upset, but the city would continue working perfectly well. If the garbage collectors went away, though, it would result in disease and social unrest, eventually leading to societal catastrophe.

It's not as easy to make the same sort of value judgment among species in nature, however. One of them could be that quiet ecological keystone, gluing ecosystems together—the one species whose removal causes the whole community to collapse. Another species could be providing a service that is essential to our survival—just as do many insects, unknown to us, as they pollinate the trees that produce the fruits we eat.

As Bob Paine said years ago, all species may be equal, but some are more equal than others—and we don't yet know which ones. But we do know that for millennia, humans have been removing top predators from the natural world. That impulse has simplified our world, because top predators tend to be the glue that keeps ecosystems together. It's only relatively recently that we have started to learn that all ecosystems on Earth are linked to one another in ways that may appear magical—because they are.

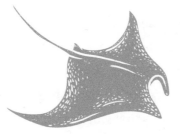

CHAPTER SEVEN

THE BIOSPHERE

I T TAKES 90 MINUTES to go around the world if you travel on the International Space Station. In that short time, everything—deserts, mountains, rivers, lakes, cities—goes by. Every astronaut who has had that experience has described how humbling it feels to look down on our little blue marble traveling in an infinite void. The sight of the atmosphere as a thin, hazy layer shows how fragile our world and our existence are. The astronauts talk about a sense of awe and wonder, a near-mystical realization of how insignificant our world is. They talk of a sense of unity. The boundaries between ecosystems, so apparent on the ground, almost disappear. Same goes for borders between countries. From up there, they appear irrelevant. We are all connected to one another, and to the natural world, of which we are part. Astronauts call it the "overview effect."

In 1974, biologists James Lovelock and Lynn Margulis encouraged us all to see our biosphere as a single living organism. They called it the "Gaia hypothesis," suggesting that the biosphere acts like a superorganism where everything is connected, where one part of the planet will compensate or regulate another part if it is in trouble, like a body with different organs that work in synchrony. In those days, many scientists and other serious thinkers considered Lovelock and Margulis had gone off the deep end. But their idea was nothing new: Traditional knowledge in many cultures already considered all of the natural world to be one interconnected and interdependent system. Since then, scientific knowledge has been revealing little by little what indigenous peoples learned through generations of experience and natural history knowledge, and what astronauts experienced by seeing our planet from space. The interconnections go from small to large, from local to global—and they do not cease to amaze me. Pull a lever, make some small change, and unexpected things will happen, especially when keystone species are involved.

Let's start small, with bacteria. *Prochlorococcus* is the scientific name of a bacterium only a millionth of a millimeter in size. It is so small that we did not discover its existence until 1988, yet it is one of the most abundant creatures on the planet. Some 20,000 of these bacteria live in a single drop of seawater. *Prochlorococcus* makes a living by using sunlight in the shallow ocean to transform carbon dioxide and nutrients in seawater into energy, releasing oxygen in the process. It is a process similar to what plants do on land: photosynthesis. Yet terrestrial plants, our forests and grasslands, produce only half of the oxygen we breathe. The other half of our planet's oxygen comes from the ocean, from seaweed on our shores, microscopic plants in the open ocean, and microbes like these *Prochlorococcus*. A little bacterium that we did not know only 30 years ago, and other marine creatures unknown to most humans, provide the oxygen in every other breath we take. These microbes are probably the smallest, yet one of the most important, foundation species on our planet—the foundation of life as we know it. Small but mighty.

Baleen whales, such as fin whales and blue whales, eat small creatures such as krill and little fish that live in the ocean shallows. Toothed whales, such as the sperm whales of *Moby-Dick* fame, eat giant squid in the ocean depths. Fishermen (and some scientists funded by the fishing industry) have argued that whales eat too much krill and fish, and that we ought to kill whales to ensure more fish for us humans. These claims are especially blatant in the ·Southern Ocean, where Japanese vessels continue to slaughter whales. But the situation has not turned out to be so simple. Fewer whales has not meant more krill and fish. In fact, as the whale population was decimated, so was that of the krill. Why?

Whales eat massive amounts of krill and small fish, which contain significant amounts of iron in their tissues. The whales absorb part of that iron but release much of it in their feces when they come to the water's surface to breathe. The phytoplankton in the ocean need iron to synthesize chlorophyll—the green pigment that absorbs sunlight during photosynthesis. Because iron does not dissolve easily in seawater, many ocean areas are iron poor. Thus, by releasing feces high in iron, whales fertilize the shallow waters, fostering the growth of phytoplankton and turning clear waters into green blooms. Krill feast on the abundant phytoplankton and bloom as well. The fish eat the krill and they increase in number, and so on and so forth—penguins, seals, whales, orcas . . .

But there is more. Whales often eat at depth. Sperm whales hunt squid more than a kilometer (3,200 ft) underwater. The up-and-down movements of diving whales mix surface and deeper waters, helping to bring more nutrients from the deep to the upper reaches of the ocean. In fact, a study estimated that marine animals cause as much ocean mixing as winds and tides together. Without the predation and mixing caused by whales, much of the krill would die and sink to the bottom, hence impoverishing the shallower waters by making their nutrients unavailable.

The point is, scientific observations have shown us that whales do not deplete the ocean of their prey. Their behavior actually helps create more phytoplankton, more krill, and more fish. In the absence of whales, in fact, the shallow offshore waters could become a desert. What we really should be asking is, How many more fish would there be if we hadn't killed so many whales?

FROM THE OCEAN FOOD WEB to the terrestrial soil: Here's another example of interdependence that nature is just now revealing to us. When we walk in a forest we see the trees, but we miss what really makes the trees—and all other plants—possible. "In many ways the ground beneath our feet is as alien as a distant planet," wrote the editors of the scientific journal *Science* in a 2004 special issue on soils. "The processes occurring in the top few centimeters of Earth's surface are the basis of all life on dry land but the opacity of soil has severely limited our understanding of how it functions." If you think this is an overstatement, wait for what comes now.

Healthy soil contains a complex, multilevel food web that self-organizes as intricately as the food web aboveground, with extraordinary diversity and an impact on all life on land. In one handful of healthy soil there are a trillion bacteria, 10,000 protozoans (single-celled creatures, such as amoebas), 10,000 roundworms, and 25 kilometers (15.5 mi) of very fine fungal filaments—in addition to the larger organisms we can see, such as earthworms and insects. The interdependencies and interactions within this underground ecological community are amazing.

On the forest floor, insects shred organic debris—dead leaves, rotten wood, the carcasses of dead rodents and birds, for example—facilitating decomposition of smaller debris by the abundant soil bacteria and adding their nutritive feces to the mix. Beneficial bacteria preempt the space and prevent pathogens from occupying the soil, in a way providing preventive health care for the plants. Round-worms and protozoans eat the bacteria and poop nitrogen back into the soil. Earthworms create microtunnels, allowing oxygen to infiltrate the soil, and deposit their feces, which also help fertilize the soil. The action of all these creatures, together with those miles of fungi filaments, form a complex web that gives structure to the soil, helping it retain water and protect plants from pathogens. Experiments have proven how necessary this soil ecosystem is for plants. Seeds thrive when grown in natural soil from a pine forest, rich with fungi and microbes; they do not survive in soil that has been sterilized.

The fungi of the underworld are some of the most underappreciated organisms on Earth. We love to eat truffles and pay crazy amounts for them, but other fungi in the soil are performing a job that is far more important, establishing the basis for a global system of ecological interconnections. Plant roots and fungi engage in one of the most important symbiotic relationships on our planet: It's called mycorrhizae—a word derived from the Greek, literally meaning "mushroom root." About 80 percent of the world's plants depend upon it. Tiny fungal filaments called mycelia, about one-sixtieth the size of a root, worm their way into tighter spaces and access the nutrients that nearby plants need, such as phosphorus and nitrogen. Through the mycorrhizae, this interdependent web of fungal and plant roots, the fungi trade nutrients in exchange for the sugars the plants produce.

In addition, fungi produce a sticky protein called glomalin, which glues the soil together and gives the soil its brown color. Gardeners and farmers call this "tilth"— that feeling of healthy, granular soil sieving through your fingers. Glomalin alone stores a third of all the carbon in our soils. Thus, these underappreciated little fungi are key in sequestering much of our atmospheric carbon pollution in the soil. Unfortunately, though, we have treated the soil as a single-use, disposable item, not recognizing it as a complex web of living things. Industrial agriculture pollutes the soil with fertilizers—excess nutrients, much of which end up in the ocean, creating dead zones—and pesticides, killing the bacteria, fungi, and invertebrates that make it naturally productive. If we changed these practices, it could have worldwide effects. A recent study suggests that a global shift to regenerative agriculture— practices designed to produce and restore the life of the soil—would have the ability to sequester most of the excess carbon dioxide in the atmosphere.

THE EXTRAORDINARY SOIL ECOSYSTEM gives us the plants and the trees and the forests. And that's just the beginning of the story.

Suzanne Simard grew up in the forests of British Columbia. She used to spend time lying on her back, watching the majestic tree crowns reach the sky. As she explained in a beautiful TED talk that has been watched more than four million times, a short time as a forester showed her the relentless destruction of the old forests, so she went back to school to study the trees themselves. She had heard of a lab experiment that suggested a pine seedling root could transmit carbon to another pine seedling root. That could be happening in nature, too, she thought, so she decided to conduct an experiment to prove it. Funding agencies did not think highly of her idea, so she had to borrow sophisticated equipment, radioactive carbon gas, and delicate lab instruments from her university and combine them with everyday materials like plastic bags, duct tape, and shade cloth that she purchased at a department store.

Simard established an outdoor plot where she grew three species of tree—paper birch, Douglas fir, and western red cedar. She planted 80 groups of three trees, one of each species. She placed some individuals under clear plastic bags and injected the bags with different carbon isotopes—chemical elements that are marked in ways that make them easy to spot in a plant's tissues. She injected the bags containing birch with carbon dioxide made up of carbon-14, an unstable isotope that undergoes radioactive decay. She injected the Douglas fir bags with carbon dioxide made up of carbon-13, a stable isotope.

After an hour, Simard went back to the bags and ran a Geiger counter over the leaves. The birch leaves gave that classic crackling sound of the Geiger counter in the presence of radioactivity, which meant that the birch tree had absorbed the radioactive carbon dioxide through photosynthesis. She then ran the Geiger counter over the Douglas fir. Eureka! The Geiger counter crackled near the fir tree leaves as well, which meant that the radioactive carbon had passed from one plant to another. The plants were isolated inside their own bags, so the only way for the carbon to pass from the birch to the fir was underground, through the soil, via their root systems.

Noting the isotope markers, Simard actually found that carbon was transferred two ways, from the birch to the Douglas fir and vice versa. But the carbon was not exchanged haphazardly between species; there was a method to it. Trees were actually helping each other. A birch inside a plastic bag sent carbon to a nearby fir that was under a shade cloth. During the summer months, Simard discovered, adult birch trees in the sun help fir trees in the shade. But in the fall, when the birch loses its leaves but the fir still has green needles, it is the fir that sends nutrients to the birch. The key to this unbelievable underground communication network is the mycorrhizae, by which fungal mycelia connect different individual trees in the forest. Surprisingly, although birch and fir trees communicated, they did not connect with cedar trees, which must have been on a completely different network.

Simard's findings radically changed our view of forests, showing that trees are not just competitors for light and nutrients; they are cooperators. But there is more. Some trees are hubs, or mother trees, and have a greater role in

the forests than others—another type of foundation species. Mother trees can be connected to hundreds of other
trees. They nurture young seedlings growing under their
shade. Simard's experiments showed that seedlings that
receive carbon from a mother tree are four times more likely
to survive than those growing independently. One question
led to another, and Simard conducted another experiment
to test whether mother trees would recognize their kin—
seedlings developing from their own seeds. She planted
Douglas fir seedlings near their mother tree, and the results
confirmed her intuition: Mother trees would accommodate
their root growth to make space for their own seedlings,
helping them develop a wider mycorrhizae network and
sending more carbon to them than to seedlings that originated from another mother tree. If this does not seem
enough, mother trees that are injured or dying send defense
signals to their network, making younger trees more resistant to future stresses.

TREES TALKING TO EACH OTHER, feeding each other,
communicating to each other—it's like the Pandora ecosystem in the film *Avatar*. Science fiction? Not really. Let's scale
up again. We have resilient forests dependent on a complex
soil ecosystem. Where do we go from here?

There is a belief among the Yanomami people of the
Amazon Basin that the native trees of the natural forests call

the rain, while the plantation trees don't know how to do that. Many will think this is a legend—trees could not possibly call the rain! But science can show us that there is truth within this legend.

Amazonian trees absorb water from the ground and move it up to their leaves, where part of it is released into the atmosphere through the process of evapotranspiration. As that massive amount of water vapor over the vast Amazonian forest condenses and falls back to the ground as rain, it lowers the air pressure, which in turn pulls dense, moist air from over the Atlantic Ocean. This process creates a river in the sky, so to speak—a giant conveyor belt by which the forest creates its own rain, which in turn waters the forest. Experts estimate that there is more water in the river in the sky than in the Amazon River itself—notwithstanding the fact that it's the largest river on our planet. So now, should we believe the traditional knowledge of the Yanomami?

But there is more. The clouds created by and above the forest drop their load when they hit the tall mountain barrier of the Andes. The rain erodes the rocks of the Andes, which contain iron and silica, the material that makes up the sand grains on most of our beaches. That material sifts down, ultimately to the shoreline. Silica reaching the Atlantic is assimilated by phytoplankton—diatoms similar to those that bloom in the sardine run in South Africa. They use it to build their skeletons, which look like beautiful oval or round cages made of glass when viewed under a microscope.

Diatoms, like other phytoplankton, produce enormous volumes of oxygen. When they die, they sink to the bottom of the ocean where, over time and under the pressure of trillions of diatom skeletons sinking through millennia, they will become sandstone. Over geologic time—millions of years—the bottom of the sea may emerge as a desert whose sand grains are made of the silica of ancient diatoms.

That's not the end of today's story, though. Sandstorms on the Sahara push dust loaded with nutrients—like silica and iron—toward the Atlantic, and often on the 8,000-kilometer (4,970 mi) journey across it. That dust settles over the Amazonian forest and fertilizes it. It may take millions of years, but the forest is getting back some of what it sowed.

Therefore, small ecological heroes such as bacteria and fungi in the soil help trees grow, and trees form forests that call the rain, and the rain influences weather patterns worldwide that help erode the tallest mountains so that microscopic algae in the ocean will create the sand in what will become deserts millions of years later, which in turn will help fertilize the microscopic life in the forest soil. Maybe Gaia exists after all.

COMPLEX ECOSYSTEMS interconnect as one within our biosphere. Embedded in almost all of these ecosystems is the human body.

Our bodies have about 30 trillion cells. That is more cells than stars in our galaxy. I find it hard to comprehend. What's more shocking is that our bodies carry a similar number of microbes. That's 30 trillion microbes, living mostly in our gut and covering our skin. What do all these creatures do?

Let's start with breast milk. It contains complex sugar molecules—oligosaccharides—that newborn infants cannot digest. They lack the necessary enzymes, a fact that puzzled nutritionists for years. But advances in medical technologies have shown that these complex sugars are not destined for the baby but for a bacterium in the baby's gut called *Bifido-bacterium infantis*. When this bacterium is well fed, it proliferates and preempts the gut space, preventing the establishment of harmful microbes. In addition, by digesting these complex sugars, *B. infantis* releases fatty acids that feed the baby's gut cells. Finally, *B. infantis* helps maintain the integrity of the lining of the baby's intestines, which is crucial to protect it from infection and inflammation.

Most of our gut bacteria are acquired during birth, but we acquire other bacteria from dust or our pets. Recent studies have shown that children with a family dog or children who spend more time playing outside have lower rates of asthma or lung allergies than those who don't. Bacteria are also exchanged between people: As we move and exhale, we are continuously sending them out into the air—at the rate of 37 million an hour. Exposure to helpful bacteria helps our immune system and overall health. Once inside our bodies, bacterial genes can enter our own DNA through a process called lateral gene transfer. As a matter of fact, at least 145 bacterial genes have made their way into our DNA over the course of human evolution. The modern tendency to use antibiotics actually reduces the diversity and abundance of a person's naturally occurring microbes which, we are finding, brings negative consequences, including higher rates of obesity and type 2 diabetes.

Our gut bacteria help keep us healthy, body and mind. They play an important role in the synthesis of hormones, enzymes, vitamins, and molecules that influence the immune system. Some of these molecules help regulate stress and even influence our temperament. This might sound crazy: gut microbes influencing our mood? Again, a series of experiments have tested this hypothesis, first in lab rats as a precursor to clinical trials involving people. Feces—which contain living microbes from inside the gut—were taken from people with depression and people without and transplanted into rats. Rats that received the gut microbes from depressed people showed changes in behavior and metabolism characteristic of depression—reduced socializing or physical withdrawal, for example—whereas the control rats did not. These experiments showed that depression can be caused by decreased species richness and diversity in the gut microbial ecosystem. Bacteria in our guts can mediate our behavior and modulate brain development, function, and behavior.

Our world is an ecological Russian nesting doll—ecosystems within ecosystems within our larger ecosystem, the biosphere, a global self-organizing system with millions of species interconnected and interdependent at all levels. From the International Space Station, it is easy to see Earth as one single system. The interdependence of all life on Earth may be more evident from that vantage point than from here, on the ground. Yet it is essential for our future that humans experience that transcendent overview effect and begin to treat the biosphere like a living thing instead of something to ignore or abuse. We have such an overwhelming impact on the entire biosphere. Why? What type of keystone species are we?

CHAPTER EIGHT

HOW ARE WE DIFFERENT?

N MAY 2019, I jumped into the waters of Millennium Atoll, a chain of coral islands shaped like a
banana, 14 kilometers (8.7 mi) long. As soon as my
bubbles cleared, I saw a dozen gray reef sharks surrounding me. No, it didn't scare me. It brought me
great delight. They signified a thriving marine ecosystem.

As part of our National Geographic Pristine Seas project,
we have explored many such isolated and uninhabited coral
reef atolls and islands across the Pacific. Some take as many
as five days to reach from the nearest inhabited location.
Their ecosystems are as pristine as it gets because no one
lives there and no one fishes the reefs. At each of these
islands we measure the biomass of fish, from the smallest
to the largest, from little blennies to sharks. And we con-
sistently find that, in these pristine coral reefs, the top
predators account for most of the fish biomass. At the end
point of ecological succession, sharks have reached their

maximum abundance. In mature, pristine coral reefs, a landscape of fear prevails where predators are kings and prey are careful not to be too conspicuous.

In ecosystems that have not been disturbed by any humans, predators control the abundance of their prey but don't eliminate it completely. Predator and prey, eater and food, coexist, and have for millions of years—otherwise one of them, or both, wouldn't be here. As with the Canadian lynx and hare, predator and prey can oscillate: When the predator drives the prey down, predator numbers will go down, then prey numbers will go up again, and so on and so forth.

But human exploitation of species tends to produce a different pattern: As we become the predator, the abundance of our prey goes down, and often goes extinct, while the human population keeps increasing. The last Caribbean monk seal was observed south of Jamaica in 1952; the last passenger pigeon—whose giant flocks of billions of birds once darkened the skies of North America—was named Martha, and she died in 1914 at the Cincinnati Zoo. These, and many other species, are gone forever, now only to be observed as specimens dried, embalmed, or in jars in museum collections.

But humans drive species *ecologically extinct* as well. That is, if prey are not totally wiped from the face of Earth, their numbers become so low that they can't perform their ecological roles anymore. In other words, they become ecologically irrelevant. Examples include the Mediterranean monk seal, which numbers less than 500 individuals in the entire sea, and the freshwater mussel *Unio foucauldianus,* of which only between 100 and 500 individuals are estimated to remain in southern Morocco. The Mediterranean monk seal is not exerting its former top predator role across the Mediterranean, nor is the freshwater mussel population filtering as much freshwater as it formerly did. Ecological extinction is the last step before global extinction.

In fact, humans are driving species extinct at a rate at least a thousand times faster than the natural background rate. There is no oscillation between us and wild species as there is between, say, the lynx and the hare. Why? Aren't we subject to the same ecological processes as the rest of life on our planet?

At a scientific conference, my friend Boris Worm, a German professor of marine ecology who teaches at Dalhousie University in Canada, posed a question to Bob Paine: "If the sea otter and the *Pisaster* starfish are keystone species in the Pacific Northwest, what are we?" To which Bob replied, "We're hyperkeystone predators."

Boris and Bob agreed to co-write a paper on this idea. They reviewed the scientific literature and found that humans exploit terrestrial herbivores—mostly even-toed ungulates such as wild pigs, peccaries, hippopotamuses, llamas, deer, giraffes, antelopes, and wild sheep and goats—at a level similar to that of other predators. What distinguishes us from other predators, however, is that we exploit terrestrial carnivores and top predators—wolves, lynxes, lions, and tigers, for example—at rates four to 10 times higher than other species. Even more shocking, we exploit prey in the ocean at rates 11 to 15 times greater than those of other species. No matter where in the food web those marine species are found—from the humble sardine to the mighty white shark—humans kill all marine species at disproportionately higher rates than any of their other predators.

Some of the species we deplete are keystone species, which means that our impacts cascade across entire ecosystems. We currently sit at the top of a global food web that touches virtually every other species on Earth (save microbes living deep in Earth's crust). We're wrecking ecosystems across the planet by removing the key species on top of each food web. The building of ecosystems is asymmetrical: It takes decades, centuries, or even millennia to accumulate structure and information in the slow crawl toward ecological maturity—and yet, as we have observed too often, all that information can be lost in a matter of hours.

The Library of Alexandria was the largest repository of knowledge in the ancient world. It took centuries for scholars and philosophers to accumulate all that knowledge. About 2,000 years ago, the library burned down within hours, and with it, most of the knowledge of ancient philosophers and scientists, which will never be available again. We might have rediscovered some of what was lost in the ashes, but imagine what the world could be today if we had preserved that ancient wisdom.

The same can be said for natural ecosystems. A tropical forest in Borneo is home to tens of thousands of species of plants and animals, living in a complex web of interdependencies. Within just a few days, a corporation can send in bulldozers that will replace the forest with a palm tree monoculture. All that genetic information, that baroque complexity of nature, the millions of interactions between species, and all the services they provide to us will be gone—forever. And as with the Library of Alexandria, the loss of that information will reverberate through the generations, whether anyone recognizes it or not.

On land, habitat destruction is actually the main driver of biodiversity loss. (In the ocean, it is fishing, the largest hunting operation on the planet.) Over half of the land on Earth has been transformed to feed us or build our cities. Agriculture and livestock operations have transformed half of the habitable land and use 75 percent of our available freshwater. In the United States alone, 41 percent of the land in the lower 48 states is used to raise livestock. All these operations represent massive examples of habitat destruction. Whether an ancient rainforest is clear-cut in Indonesia or Malaysia to make way for a palm oil plantation or a pristine grassland in the American Midwest is turned into a cornfield or a grazing range measuring tens of thousands of acres, it results in catastrophic biodiversity loss. As we saw earlier, ecological succession is a process that takes a long time, requiring a series of steps by which energy accumulated during one stage is used to facilitate the development of the next. Nature nurtures ecological succession, but we humans are responsible for the regression of ecosystems.

To add insult to injury, we are now wiping out species not only directly, by hunting and destroying habitats, but also by more indirect ways. Poisoning is one example of our indirect influence.

Whalers drove the large whales to near extinction in the 20th century, forcing orcas to move closer to shore and eat sea lions and sea otters. But orcas are now victims of another long tentacle of the human influence on the ocean. A recent study suggests that half of the orca populations worldwide will collapse by 2050–2060 because of toxic chemicals that were banned 30 years ago. Polychlorinated biphenyls, or PCBs, are compounds that were used in paints, coolants, and capacitors. In the mid-1970s, acknowledging that PCBs probably caused cancer in humans, governments banned them. Yet PCBs are still among us, in legacy products including transformers and some ship paints. PCBs are long-lived. They break down very slowly and seep into the environment, where they enter the food web, eaten by small animals. Because orcas are at the top of that food web (under our high throne) and eat many contaminated prey, they accumulate PCBs in their blubber. Now they are among the most contaminated animals on our planet, their immune systems and their ability to reproduce damaged irreparably by PCBs. That might be good news for the sea otters, but the large Pacific Northwest ocean food web will be less complex and less healthy as the orca population declines.

Acoustic pollution is another indirect influence we humans exert on the natural world. From the deafening noise in a metropolitan subway station or airport to the constant hum produced by cities that can be heard many miles away, it is almost impossible to find places where we can just enjoy natural sounds—or near silence. A recent study shows that even in the national parks and nature reserves, we cannot escape from our noise. In 63 percent of the protected area units in the United States, background noise levels doubled because of human-produced sounds. In 21 percent of protected areas, human noise was 10 times the natural background noise, or even higher. These levels exceed the limits above which wildlife is significantly disturbed.

In October 2014, I was diving under an oil platform off the coast of Gabon during one of our Pristine Seas expeditions. The pylons of the platform were the only hard substrate over a muddy seafloor, and they had become an artificial reef of sorts, covered with sponges, algae, and orange cup corals. Because fishing is banned near the platform, fish from small damselfish to large snappers and tuna were abundant. The most memorable moment that day, though, was hearing something quite different: the song of the ocean sirens, the humpback whale. Eerie and hypnotic, the song of the humpback whale can be heard from dozens of miles away.

The only downside was the continuous humming, clanking, and clinking of the oil drilling operation nearby.

It bothered me during the entire dive. Oil platforms, ship noise, seismic testing, and other human-produced clatter are driving marine mammals crazy, too. Seismic air gun blasting is notoriously harmful. Looking for oil and gas deposits under the seafloor, specialized ships drop air guns into the ocean that shoot extremely loud blasts every 10 seconds for days to months at a time. These blasts can travel underwater more than 2,000 miles, disturbing the sound landscape and destroying the hearing organs of whales and dolphins, which they depend on to feed and communicate. The blue whale, the largest animal ever to inhabit our planet, produces a low-frequency song that is believed to travel thousands of miles underwater too. But the blue whale song does not kill anyone. Neither does the humpback's siren call.

Our human noises are different.

THE QUESTION STILL REMAINS: In what way are we so different? What has enabled humans to become the top keystone predator on Earth—the one hyperkeystone predator, as Bob Paine called us?

Anthropologists will rightly say that our complex brain has allowed humans to develop language and hunt in groups. But so do marine mammals. Humpback whales eat krill and small fish in the shallow ocean by swimming sideways or from below up toward the surface, opening their massive mouths to capture 5,000 gallons of water and everything in it. But often their prey is too dispersed, and here is where whale teamwork comes in handy. A handful of humpbacks dive around their prey, and as they swim back up to the surface, each whale exhales, creating a circular curtain of air bubbles that scares the prey into the middle. Then the whales only have to breach the surface with their big mouths agape, and they get a lot of prey in a single gulp. Teamwork in action. Similarly, wolves hunt deer in packs in Yellowstone National Park, lions hunt zebra together in the Serengeti, and sea lions team up on yellowfin tuna in a shallow bay in the Galápagos Islands.

Could the difference be our toolmaking abilities? For a long time, people thought humans were the only animals that use tools. We built spears to kill animals larger than us, plows to till the soil and plant domesticated crops, nets to catch a lot of fish at a time, and so on. Those extra appendages allowed humans to kill more and produce more of everything they needed.

But other animals also use tools. Jane Goodall famously found that chimpanzees use twigs to catch termites in Tanzania, and researchers have discovered the same patterns in chimpanzees in other African countries. Charles Darwin had already written in his *Descent of Man* in 1871 that chimpanzees used stones to crack nuts, orangutans used sticks as levers, and baboons used stones to attack individuals of another baboon species. Sea otters use stones to break open their sea urchin prey. Dolphins in Shark Bay, Australia, use marine sponges to protect their beaks while they search for food on the seafloor. New Caledonian crows use twigs and wood (and sometimes metal wire) as probes to impale larvae. And there are many more examples of other animals using tools. But the big difference is that they don't drive other species extinct, and we do.

A few humans with opposable thumbs and modern tools may not be able to wreak havoc on a planetary scale, but our rapid population growth pushes our influence way beyond any individual impact. The Chinese, for example, eat relatively small amounts of fish, and they eat species that are relatively low in the food web. One might say, then, that China has one of the smallest per capita effects on fish populations. But multiply that per capita effect times 1.4 billion, the population of China, and it becomes the country with the largest impact on ocean fish populations.

Nature shows us plenty of examples of alternating predator and prey—the lynx-hare type of dynamic—but that pattern somehow does not seem to apply to humans. Why don't our numbers go down when the availability of our prey goes down? To explore that question, we need to talk about energy.

Most natural ecosystems are limited in their growth by the energy of the sun and the availability of resources—in other words, nutrients. Every day, the Earth's surface receives 120,000 terawatts of solar energy, or 175 watts per square meter. If you aren't an energy expert (and I am not), these numbers might not mean much to you, but we can put it another way: Every hour and a half, the sun strikes Earth's surface with enough energy to power human civilization for a year. The energy we intercept from the sun in 30 days is equivalent to all the world's fossil fuels combined, both those we have already burned and those still in the world's untapped underground reserves.

Plants can put that solar energy to use by using very small natural machines—the molecular engine inside the microscopic chloroplasts in their leaves that accomplishes photosynthesis. Combining sunlight with water, carbon dioxide, and nutrients, plants generate carbohydrates—the organic material that provides the food and three-dimensional structure at the foundation of entire ecosystems.

Plants produce organic material at an average rate of 0.21 watt per square meter—on average, only 0.13 percent of the solar energy available to them (although individual plants can have efficiencies of up to 4 percent). Plants might not be very efficient in their use of solar energy, but they do produce enough to support the entire living envelope of our planet—our biosphere.

In the same way that a person's weight will be the product of how many calories eaten minus how many calories burned every day, the total biomass of a terrestrial ecosystem will depend on how much plant biomass is consumed minus how much is respired—that is, burned up in activities such as growth and cell development. In the case of a food web with several levels, plant biomass will determine how much herbivore biomass there can be; herbivore biomass will determine how much carnivore biomass there can be;

and all animal biomass will determine how much top predator biomass there can be. Just as the weight of a person will depend partly on how much food is in the kitchen, the total biomass of the ecosystem will depend on available plant biomass. Top predators cannot develop a biomass that cannot be supported by the available food.

But this calculus does not seem to apply to humans. We come back to our question: Why don't humans follow the same regulatory rules as other predators and preys? Why are we wiping out every other species while our population keeps increasing? Here is the answer: Because we have found a way to unshackle ourselves from the daily limitations of nonhuman ecosystems. In other words, not only do we use energy from the present, thanks to the solar energy striking us daily, but we also use energy from the past.

Professor Ramón Margalef, the father of Spanish ecology and a poet among scientists, wrote about human impacts in a dispassionate way beginning as early as the 1970s. When I was a student of biology at the University of Barcelona in the late 1980s, he was in his last years of academic life, yet he still went almost every day to his little windowless office in the ecology department, which he had founded in 1967. He was a tall man, typically wearing a shirt and tie tucked under a V-neck sweater and a jacket. His demeanor was gentle, and his face drew a permanent smile. He was a man of another time, always calling his colleagues "Dr. So-and-so." Everyone called him Dr. Margalef. I was privileged enough to have sat in on a handful of his lectures.

How Are We Different?

When I was conducting my Ph.D. work in the early 1990s, studying the recovery of the marine ecosystem in the Medes Islands Marine Reserve, I witnessed very few—and small—fish outside the reserve. I was just beginning to realize the full extent of our human destructive power, and it perplexed me. So one day I approached Margalef in his office—he always had time for students—and asked him what makes us such a powerful predator. His smile deepened, and he answered: "The necrosphere."

The necrosphere, from the Greek word *nekrós,* meaning "dead." The biosphere is the living layer of our planet; the necrosphere is the dead layer. It includes everything that was alive and is not anymore: the leaves that fall in the autumn and litter the forest floor, or a whale that dies and falls to the deep sea. The recent necrosphere is constantly in limbo. Dead matter is quickly recycled by scavengers: bacteria, fungi, and animals that eat detritus. Those colorful autumn leaves that fall on the forest floor will be consumed right then and there, their constituent parts reintegrated into the food web. An ant cutting a leaf will be eaten by a little bird, which will be eaten by a weasel, which will be eaten by a red fox. Whatever is not immediately taken up into the food web will be reused by worms and fungi and become part of the rich soil that will nurture the trees.

In the sea, a pod of orcas may kill a gray whale and eat only its tongue—apparently a delicacy for orcas. Then they will abandon the corpse. The tongueless dead body (perhaps somewhat damaged by hungry sharks) will eventually sink to the ocean floor. In the nutrient-poor deep sea, the whale carcass will foster its own ecological succession: First mobile scavengers such as deep-sea sharks, ratfish, and hagfish will smell the corpse and come consume the flesh in the same way that lions and vultures eat the meat of a dead zebra. This first stage in the whale fall succession can last a few months. Once the flesh has gone to fatten up the large scavengers of the deep, smaller animals—worms, mollusks, and crustaceans—will eat whatever blubber is left, including any that has seeped into the mud around the whale. This phase can last a couple of years. Soon all that remains of the whale is its skeleton. With the help of bacteria, bone-eating worms will break down the fats and oils inside the bones, generating sulfur that in turn attracts other types of bacteria and filter-feeding animals like mussels. A few decades later, nothing will remain of the whale but a thin, light stain on the dark seafloor. Even this part of the necrosphere will eventually be recycled and become part of the biosphere again.

On land and in the sea, these examples showcase a key difference between human-built and other ecosystems: Other species don't produce and accumulate waste. Everything is reused or repurposed in nonhuman ecosystems. The natural world is the perfect circular economy, where everything, even after its lifetime, becomes a source for something else.

THERE IS A PART OF THE NECROSPHERE that does not decompose and is therefore not turned into living organisms: We might call it the ancient necrosphere. Its most conspicuous distinguishing characteristic is that it is made up of organisms that were quickly buried at the bottom of the ocean or in peatbogs after dying, making them inaccessible to other species. Over time, these sediments continue to accumulate, burying that dead matter deeper and deeper. The extreme heat and pressure on top of these dead organisms eventually turns them into coal, natural gas, or oil—the things we now call fossil fuels. Fossil fuels are energy from the past—once sunlight—that now fuel our society. Other forms of life use the recent necrosphere, but only humans have learned to use the ancient one.

For humans, the ancient necrosphere is the key that unlocked the shackles of the present and allowed us to escape the alternating turnover cycle of predator and prey. We cheat: We use energy from the past to subsidize our over-exploitation of the present. That energy subsidy allows us to build artificial ecosystems (cities) that consume more energy (including food) than they produce. No other species can do that. Had we continued to use daily solar energy as our main source of energy (via plant biomass and natural food webs), the human population would probably never have reached the current seven and a half billion (and growing). The world would be a different place. To be clear, I'm not making a judgment or attempting to romanticize about what could have been a different path. I'm just making an observation.

The truth is that we are acting as though we had more than one planet Earth. The Global Footprint Network, a think tank, has estimated that in 2019 we had used up all of Earth's annual productivity by July 29—the earliest ever. That is, in less than eight months we exhausted Earth's budget for the year. What did we do in the remaining four months? We ate away from the principal, with the help of energy from the ancient necrosphere. One does not need to be an economist to know what will happen to a savings account if we keep depleting the principal. We are able to overuse Earth's resources in great part because of our use of past solar energy stored underground as fossil fuels. We use energy from the past to subsidize our looting of the present.

The burning of the necrosphere has not only helped us destroy biodiversity at a global scale; it has also filled our fragile atmosphere with too much carbon pollution. The carbon dioxide and other greenhouse gases that human activities emit have been accumulating at dangerous levels, which has caused the most rapid elevation in air and sea-water temperatures ever recorded on Earth. The countries of the world agreed in December 2015 in Paris to reduce our emissions so that global temperatures do not exceed an average 2°C (3.6°F) (ideally, 1.5°C/2.7°F) relative to preindustrial times. But the Paris Climate Agreement will not be achievable if we continue depleting biodiversity worldwide, as we will see later.

Humans are different from every other top predator on the planet because of a variety of reasons: superior intelligence, dexterity, teamwork, language, and many other factors. But the key reason that makes us a hyperpredator is that we have discovered how to use the ancient necrosphere. Is there a problem with that? Some argue that we humans have never been wealthier and healthier, and that the world economy keeps growing, so what's the problem? Do we really need all that biological diversity? Isn't it more important to grow our GDP?

Soil is the basis of life on land. Healthy soils harbor a labyrinthine network of fungi that provide nutrients to plants in exchange for sugars. The unfarmed soil in the American Midwest supports tall prairie grasses and sequesters a great deal of carbon. The sunflower roots in the photo are six feet deep.

Coral reefs, as here in Palau, are called the "rainforests of the sea" because they contain more species than any other marine ecosystem. Exploitation and global heating are turning these lush underwater gardens into graveyards.

The Amazon forest not only contains hundreds of thousands of species of plants and animals but also generates its own weather and rain. Losing more than 20 percent of the current forest would turn it into a savanna.

The forest of Bialowieza, straddling the border between Poland and Belarus, is one of the last ancient—or old-growth—forests left in Europe, and one of the few ecosystems in the continent that is still home to wolves and European bison.

Urban environments are the extreme example of man-made ecosystems. Since cities like New York, pictured here, do not produce enough food or energy to support themselves, they depend on exploiting other ecosystems around the world.

Every year, billions of sardines aggregate off the coast of South Africa, thanks to the high productivity of these waters. Following the sardines are the predators, including sharks, sea lions, dolphins, and whales. Abundant predators indicate a healthy ocean ecosystem.

In the mid-1990s, Cabo Pulmo in Baja California, Mexico, was overfished and looked like an underwater barren (top). Local fishermen decided to ask the Mexican government to create a national park in the sea—a no-take marine reserve, 70 square kilometers (27 sq mi). In 10 years, Cabo Pulmo self-restored to a pristine state, including the return of the large predators like sharks, groupers, and jacks (bottom). Now those visionary fishermen are making far more money from diving tourism inside the reserve—and better fishing around it.

In 1807, Prussian naturalist Alexander von Humboldt published Naturgemalde, *aka the Chimborazo Map, the first description of plant distribution at different elevations. Humboldt's observations laid the ground for ecosystem science.*

Gipfel des Cotopaxi

Gipfel des Pico von Orizava oder Citlaltepetl

Höhe des Montblanc, zu welcher Saussure gelangt ist, im Jahr 1787.

Höhe der Stadt Quito

Höhe des Vesuvs.

Region der unterirdischen Pflanzen

Palm oil plantations like these in Borneo are infamous examples of biodiversity loss. Rainforests are razed and replaced with a monoculture that provides none of the ecosystem services of an intact rainforest.

*The intertidal zone, a boundary between land and sea, is where my friend and colleague Bob Paine discovered that keystone predators like the ochre sea star (*Pisaster ochraceus, *visible here) keep ecosystems together.*

Natural grasslands with native herbivores such as the American bison in Yellowstone National Park (top) are home to many species of plants and animals. Healthy prairie soils store large amounts of carbon and retain rainwater, thus protecting against floods. But when native herbivores are replaced with livestock, the result tends to be overgrazing and soil depletion and eventually even soil loss (bottom). Livestock occupy 77 percent of global agricultural land but produce less than 20 percent of the world's calorie supply.

The biosphere—Earth's living layer—is a single ecosystem where all life-forms are connected in some way, from the bacteria in our guts to the rainforests producing rain. Viewed from space, all man-made boundaries disappear.

Large predators can help mitigate the impacts of global heating. Tiger sharks in Shark Bay, Australia, create a "landscape of fear"—areas that dugongs avoid. Without their grazing, seagrasses can keep growing and storing carbon.

The Medes Islands off L'Estartit, Catalonia, harbor a no-take marine reserve with one of the largest concentrations of marine life in the Mediterranean. Visitors from all over Europe dive here and contribute to the local economy.

Mangroves are a miracle of nature: These trees grow in seawater, capture 10 times more carbon than tropical forests, provide a nursery for many species of commercial fish and invertebrates, and protect shores from storms.

Forests contain an invisible network of
connections. Trees can exchange nutrients
and sugars and relay stress signals with
one another thanks to the help of a complex underground web of fungi.

Douglas fir
(hub tree)

Douglas fir
(younger tree)

Douglas fir
(seedling)

Excess sugar from photosynthesis

Symbiotic
fungal network

Resource pathways

→ Sugar from trees
→ Nutrients from soil
→ Mixed resources from network:
   nutrients and carbon (from sugar)
→ Chemical stress signals

Nitrogen, potassium,
phosphorus, and
other nutrients

*Enlarged section
of tree root tip*

Resource-
exchange
pathway

Fungal
thread

Tree
root cell

(A) Network map

Hub tree

Fungal network

Younger tree

30 ft

(B) Hub trees removed
47% connections lost

All distances are to scale; tree diameters shown at larger scale.

Western spruce budworm

Paper birch

Douglas fir (hub tree)

Chemical stress signals

Ponderosa pine

Symbiotic fungal network

FOREST IN DISTRESS

Once a commercial farm, now Knepp Wildland in West Sussex, England, "rewilded" by its owners, is home to a complex ecosystem including many species of birds and large herbivores like the red deer in the photo.

The cutthroat trout in the Yellowstone River, shown here, was a reliable food source for bears, otters, and large birds, but its survival was threatened by the introduction of a nonnative trout species used for sportfishing.

After a court case spearheaded by local Maori tribes, the Whanganui River in New Zealand was granted personhood in 2017 by an act of parliament. The Whanganui is now recognized as an indivisible and living being.

There are about a thousand mountain gorillas left on Earth, and their population is recovering thanks to conservation efforts in Rwanda, the Democratic Republic of the Congo, and Uganda—work funded in part by ecotourism, which also provides local jobs.

CHAPTER NINE

DIVERSITY IS GOOD

IN DECEMBER 2002, the Scripps Institution of Oceanography hosted a conference, funded by the Sloan Foundation, on the "Knowns, Unknowns, and Unknowables of Marine Biodiversity." One of the goals was to assess the value of biodiversity and the cost of not knowing how many species there are and what they all do in nature. Through the first two days, scientist after scientist debated two conflicting philosophies. One contingent said the most important thing to do was to acquire new knowledge, while the other wanted to find ways to use the knowledge we already had to reverse the loss of marine biodiversity. The tension frustrated some participants, who were not used to thinking about the unknowable. But the most frustrated person in the 200-person auditorium may have been Natasha Loder, a reporter from *The Economist,* who finally stood up and said, "I have been sitting here for two days. I've heard many of you say that ocean biodiversity is very important, that we need to conduct more studies . . . but I have not heard anyone say yet *why* biodiversity is important. I would love to go back to my desk and write a piece for my magazine, but you guys are not helping me."

Boris Worm—who by that time had produced some of the most important studies on marine conservation—and I were sitting together just a few rows in front of Loder. We looked at each other and almost simultaneously said, "This is ridiculous. We need to find a clear and definitive answer to that question."

Boris and I decided to move quickly. We applied for a grant at the National Center for Ecological Analysis and Synthesis (NCEAS), a wonderful institution associated with the University of California, Santa Barbara. NCEAS is like catnip for ecologists. If your application is successful, you will be funded to conduct a series of workshops with colleagues of your choosing, inviting them to discuss and analyze an issue of your choosing, and working together to come up with a synthesis of your ideas. Working groups typically last two years and result in the publication of a major scientific paper. The good news is that NCEAS decided to fund us, and thus we put together a group of mostly young marine ecologists, mostly old friends, and started in earnest.

Meetings at NCEAS are so much fun. A group of passionate scientists get together for three or four days at a time a couple of times a year. Our daily schedule consisted of presentations and discussions from nine in the morning to noon. Then we walked outside to have lunch, and were back in the conference room at 1:30 p.m. At 5 p.m., our brains full of ideas, we moved to the James Joyce Pub, where we drank Guinness and talked about everything from art to soccer to coral reefs until 6:30 p.m., when we'd have dinner at a restaurant nearby. After dinner we all went back to our hotel and collapsed, happy after a fulfilling day that had fed our brains and souls. After each meeting, everyone went home with a task: compiling experimental studies on ecosystem functioning, analyzing global fishing data, or thinking of how to present the data—all to answer Loder's question: Why is marine biodiversity important? Or, more to her point, why is marine biodiversity important for humans?

We already knew that the ocean produces half of the oxygen in the atmosphere, that living coral reefs and mangroves protect our shores from the destructive effect of storm waves, that the ocean gives us food, and so on and so forth. Those details were not in question. But until then, no one had measured how important marine biodiversity is in providing all these human benefits. Thus our question became: Does more biodiversity equal more benefits? And, conversely, does the loss of biodiversity mean the loss of benefits?

WE AGREED on what we meant by biodiversity, but we needed to come to an agreement on what measure of biodiversity to use. Biodiversity is the variety of life on our planet. Biodiversity includes genetic differences within species (think of domestic dog species—yes, all dogs, from chihuahuas to shepherds, belong to just one species). It can mean differences between species—dogs and cats, for example. And finally, it can mean differences across ecosystems, such as a pine forest compared with a wetland. Biodiversity is not a simple quantifiable concept like temperature or distance, but rather it has several dimensions and can thus be measured in different ways.

The most commonly used measure of biodiversity is species richness, which simply means the number of species in one place. But that measure alone does not tell us how healthy an ecosystem is. For example, think of a pristine coral reef and an overfished coral reef. The pristine reef might have dozens of gray reef sharks, whereas the overfished reef could have just one shark left. In terms of species richness, "reef sharks" count the same in each location. Reef sharks? Check. So we could end up with the same measure of species richness on reefs that are vastly different and far apart on the maturity scale.

Ecologists have developed a better way to measure the variety of life in an ecosystem: the concept of diversity, or ecodiversity. Diversity is a measure of how species are distributed within an ecosystem. It uses the number of individuals or the biomass of a species to represent the relative abundance of that species in its ecosystem. In other words, a diversity assessment considers how evenly or equitably species numbers are distributed in a given place.

To give a couple of examples: A natural history museum—or Noah's ark—would score at the top of the diversity scale, since those would be the only places where all species are equally represented: two individuals per species, a female and a male. But an ecosystem like that could never work in nature. Imagine New York City with just two doctors, two nurses, two teachers, two taxi drivers, two pizzamakers, two garbage collectors, two canine stylists, and so on and so forth. Definitely not a functional city. In the same way, a functional coral reef will have different abundances for every species of coral, worm, sponge, and fish. The distribution of abundances will depend on the type of ecosystem, the number of species in that ecosystem, the productivity of the habitat, and the maturity of the ecosystem, among many other factors. A general rule is that a more mature ecosystem will contain more species and hence will exhibit greater diversity.

Other measures of biodiversity include the different roles that species play in an ecosystem (predator, habitat creator, or decomposer, for example) and the degree of symmetry of the boundary between ecosystems (for example, the oak forest turning into a pine forest on the mountain slope of Corsica). This complexity of units and scales makes it impossible to assess biodiversity using a single measure. It can also make it confusing for people, including biodiversity experts! But we in our NCEAS working group firmly believed that as long as we were clear about what we were measuring and what our goals were, we could answer the important questions about the value of marine biodiversity.

We were surprised, though, by how little information was available on these aspects of the ocean. We collated published studies on local experiments, long-term regional observations, and global fisheries data. We systematically searched major scientific journals from 1960 to 2005 for marine or estuarine experiments that measured any indicators of biodiversity. For example, three American scientists had conducted an experiment at the Tijuana River National Estuarine Research Reserve, just north of the United States–Mexico border. Their goal was to figure out which had a larger biomass: a marsh with more species or a marsh with fewer. They established plots with zero, one, three, or six plant species in them and observed the plots over three years. Their experiments showed that the plots containing more species accumulated more plant biomass and more nitrogen—a key nutrient. The plots with six species had almost double the plant biomass as the plots with just one species. Furthermore, the plots with more plant biomass had more complex three-dimensional structures, more microhabitats for invertebrates, more food for birds and fish, and so on and so forth. In other words, the more species of plants in the marsh, the more of everything else there was. Experiments elsewhere showed that experimental plots with more biodiversity at all levels (from number of species to genetic diversity to number of ecological functions) were more stable and more resilient, able to withstand perturbations and bounce back afterward. Other experiments tested how biodiversity manifested itself in diets and found that more diverse diets optimized fecundity, growth, survival, and the movement of energy up the food web. In short, the more biodiverse an ecosystem, and the greater the diversity of functions the ecosystem supports, the better and more efficiently it functions.

To test whether these small-scale results scaled up in time and space, we compiled data on coastal and estuarine ecosystems and from other sources. We were able to obtain data from 12 regions in Europe, North America, and Australia, along a gradient of human impact, including areas where biodiversity had been depleted, had collapsed, or had gone extinct, and places where biodiversity had recovered. Comparing places along that gradient showed that coastal and estuarine regions with more biodiversity support better fisheries, and provide a healthier nursery habitat for many species, including commercial fish. In addition, more biodiversity meant that invertebrates such as mussels, oysters, and sponges were able to filter much more water and improve the health of these ecosystems. In contrast, places that had lost much of their biodiversity suffered several times more harmful algal blooms and fish kills, with the resulting beach and shellfish closures—some as long as 35 years. Regions with reduced biodiversity also suffered almost 10 times more species invasions, and significantly greater risk of coastal flooding, because the "natural infrastructure" such as wetlands that are able to retain vast amounts of excess water was gone.

Moving to larger scales, we analyzed global fishing trends, using national fisheries statistics since 1950. Countries report their catches to the Food and Agriculture Organization of the United Nations (FAO), but there is a great deal of variety in the quality of the data. For example, industrial fishing data are more readily available than small-scale artisanal fishing. Typically, countries tend to underreport their catch. Aware of this problem, my friend Daniel Pauly, a renowned professor at the University of British Columbia, led a monumental process to "reconstruct" those catch data. Collaborating with an army of local researchers around the world, Daniel and colleagues were able to obtain data on previously unreported fisheries (small-scale fisheries, for example) and revised the data reported for industrial fisheries. The FAO statistics showed that global marine catches increased steadily since 1950, peaking in 1996 at 86 million metric tons and then slightly declining. But Daniel's reconstructed catch data disputed that paradigm: The new data showed that the global catch had actually peaked at 130 million metric tons and has been declining more sharply since 1996. We reached "peak fish" 24 years ago.

We looked at how many of those fisheries had collapsed—that is, commercial species whose abundance at sea had been depleted below 10 percent of their original abundance—since 1950. A third of the exploited fish populations had already collapsed as of 2003. As predicted by data at smaller scales, the collapses were much more frequent in ecosystems with fewer species, while the average catches and the speed of species recovery after depletion were both higher in species-rich ecosystems. In other words, the same level of fishing effort would be more likely to degrade a marine ecosystem faster in a species-poor environment than in an environment with more species.

As our work came to a conclusion, the team believed we had done what we were supposed to do. We posed a question—Why is marine biodiversity good for us?—and we tried to answer it using all available information. We mined the scientific literature for ways to make any link between biodiversity and ecosystem benefits and services. We looked for patterns across regions with different species richness and confirmation that the patterns we observed occurred at different levels of biodiversity.

The results were clear. The more biodiversity, the more benefits a marine ecosystem provides for us: better and more resilient fisheries, flood protection, cleaner coastal water, less incidence of disease because of contaminated fish and shellfish, and so on and so forth. Therefore, when human activities reduce biodiversity, they also reduce the ability of the ocean to provide for us. That was something that we thought evident, but we finally had hard evidence to prove it, and to satisfy those who don't have the benefit of intuition gained by years of experience in the field.

THERE WAS ONE MORE important question to answer: Can we recover ecosystem benefits once they have been depleted? Protecting a pristine place is a way to maintain the benefits that place provides, but what was not so clear was whether we could revive a degraded ecosystem and bring back all the services it once could yield. That would mean the difference between hope and despair.

Independent studies show that no-take marine reserves where fishing is prohibited have a biomass of fish on average six times greater, with 21 percent more species, than unprotected areas nearby. And the fish are, on average, a third larger. In short, protecting marine waters increases biodiversity within their boundaries.

Our analysis also showed that recovering biodiversity inside marine reserves helped to improve the fisheries around them. Around the areas studied, fishers caught four times more fish, on average, for the same amount of effort. Tourism revenue also increased significantly—because divers want to see fish, not empty water, and thus more visitors flock to marine reserves. We concluded that it is still possible to recover lost biodiversity, and that such recovery will likely be followed by increased productivity and more stability, which in turns means better fish catches around reserves and higher non-extractive revenue (tourism) within them.

Diversity Is Good

SO THAT'S ONE STEP: We can bring depleted ecosystems back to healthy biodiversity. But what if we push diversity to the extreme? What happens to vastly transformed ecosystems like the mass-production agricultural fields that feed us and our feedlot animals? Is there any chance of recovering biodiversity there, and is there any value in doing so?

In 1998, an international team of scientists, led by Zhu Youyong of Yunnan Agricultural University in China, set up an ambitious study to answer a simple question: Can diversity in rice varieties protect the crop from diseases? Rice is affected by a fungus that causes blast, a disease also known as rice rotten neck. The fungus kills the tip of the rice plant as it starts to flower, damaging it before it produces the grain. Yunnan Province was an ideal experimental site since it has a cool, wet climate that harbors fungus and fosters blast epidemics. Zhu and his colleagues engaged thousands of Yunnan rice farmers to participate in their experiment.

Sticky rice varieties command higher prices in the market, but they are highly susceptible to blast disease. Nonsticky hybrid rice varieties are less susceptible, so at that time 98 percent of the area's rice was grown as a monoculture: rows and rows of one or the other of two nonsticky hybrid varieties.

For the experiment, some fields were planted with a monoculture of sticky rice, some with a monoculture of hybrid rice, and some with a mix of the two, following a pattern already used by some farmers to obtain a minimum yield of sticky rice for the local market: one row of sticky rice flanked by two rows of hybrid rice on each side.

The results were very clear: Twenty percent of the sticky rice in the monoculture fields contracted blast disease, but only one percent of the sticky rice plants in the mixed fields were affected. But there is more: Grain production rates of sticky rice in the mixed fields were on average 89 percent greater than those in monoculture. Taking all factors into account, mixed populations produced more total grain per hectare than the monocultures. Another example of the value we gain from biodiversity.

IN SCIENCE, it is not always easy to provide an answer to a question as simple as the one Natasha Loder posed: Why is biodiversity important? It took years to scan the scientific literature and conduct our own analyses before we had a strong, solid response, but we can now answer her question based on the evidence of science. Simply put, the more biodiversity ecosystems have, the more productive, stable, and resilient they are—and the more benefits we obtain from them. Even agriculture benefits from crop diversity.

It would be easy for someone to argue that that's a no-brainer. Doesn't every successful long-term investor tell us that we have to diversify our portfolio to increase our returns? But our established agricultural practices of industrial monoculture do not seem to be following that obvious analogy. Be that as it may, investing in biodiversity—that is, preventing further decline and restoring as much as possible—is essential for the future of humanity. Natural ecosystems are both our savings accounts and our life insurance policies. We need to ensure that our natural capital portfolio is well diversified.

Now the question is, How do we restore our natural capital?

CHAPTER TEN

PROTECTED AREAS

TELEVISION PUSHED ME to the ocean. I grew up in the 1970s watching *The Undersea World of Jacques Cousteau* on Spanish television. Back then, there were only two TV channels, and Cousteau was the only one bringing the ocean into our living rooms. Every Sunday evening I'd sit in front of what's still called in Spain *la caja tonta*—the dumb box—eagerly waiting 20 minutes before the show started. That was before streaming and videocassettes, so I had to make sure I would not miss a second of it. As soon as the familiar theme song started to play, I asked everyone in my family to be quiet. They would join me, as glued to the screen as I was. Cousteau and his team of daring underwater explorers on board the famous *Calypso* made me dream about exotic places, about undersea wonderlands full of spectacular creatures, about divers in their cool wet suits making discovery after discovery. That's what I wanted to do with my life: Be an ocean explorer and dive among large groupers, seals, dolphins, and whales; hover over lush coral reefs with impossible color palettes; swim through kelp forests that looked like underwater cathedrals; and thrill to the possibilities that every new day would bring.

During the summer months, my parents, younger brother, and I would migrate to the Mediterranean shores, to the Costa Brava, where my dad worked. My mom, brother, and I would visit the long sandy beach or rocky coves nearby every single day. I would paddle around in my little blue fins, round black mask, and orange snorkel until I was shaking of cold. Then I'd come back to the beach, lie down on my towel, and let the sun raise my body temperature. When I was warm again, I returned to the sea. Enric, the little marine iguana.

As exciting as it was to swim in the Mediterranean waters, I was puzzled. Nowhere to be seen were the seals, dolphins, or large groupers that Cousteau showed us on TV. All I saw were a few wrasses and damselfish smaller than my mask. The bottom offered no epic kelp forests, but barren rock with sea urchins instead. Once in a while, a purple jellyfish would drift by, with the threat of a painful sting. That was the ocean that I grew up knowing.

Years later, one dive changed everything.

When I turned 18, I was legally allowed to scuba dive, so I enrolled in a local course with some college friends. In spring 1986, after several theory classes and a couple practice dives in a swimming pool, I took my first open water scuba dive. It was my first real attempt to emulate Cousteau. My heart was racing a hundred miles an hour. I was so excited and nervous that I used up the air in my tank in only 15 minutes. It should have lasted an hour. But those 15 minutes were my first taste of heaven.

Lucky for me, our instructor took us to the Medes Islands for this dive. It was my first introduction to a marine reserve. Fishing had been banned three years before in this protected area measuring less than 100 hectares (247 acres) in size. And now I could see, unlike the barren rocks of my childhood, the Medes Islands Marine Reserve harbored a miniature algal forest. More species of wrasse than I knew existed made their nests there, and sea breams swam by me in schools. On that dive I saw my first Mediterranean dusky grouper, a fat scorpionfish, and an octopus that surprised me—I had not seen it before it moved.

Only three years of protection had started an ecological succession that I followed over the years from that dive on. Over the next 10 years I went diving religiously in the Medes Islands every weekend, and every summer my colleagues from the University of Barcelona and I would dive there together for a few weeks, conducting the annual scientific monitoring of the marine reserve.

By every measure, everything was going up. Fish of commercial importance—grouper, sea bass, sea bream, and red mullet—boomed in number and size, now free from the intense pressure outside the reserve. Fan mussels the size of a tennis racket became common in the seagrass beds, recovering after unregulated anchoring and collection for ornamental purposes had nearly driven them to extinction. In those first years of diving I saw many spiny lobsters at every dive, their antennae popping out of crevices and overhangs on the limestone rock. I saw the precious Mediterranean red coral growing safe from the destructive pick of the coral hunters, circled by a turf of tiny white and yellow cup corals. Octopuses were large and abundant. I watched groupers increase in number and size, some reaching four feet long. All these species were fat and healthy: The Medes ecosystem provided plenty of food for them all.

I realize now that those poor Mediterranean waters where I first snorkeled as a kid excited me because that was my baseline. They were natural to me. They were all I knew. That was my normal. In those early days, I had no idea what marine life in the Mediterranean *could* be. I now know that I was suffering from the "shifting baseline syndrome," as my friend Daniel Pauly described in 1995. Daniel was referring to fisheries managers who, in the absence of historical data, adopt as the baseline for healthy fish populations what they encountered at the beginning of their careers. But our human fishing practices started to deplete the sea long before we started to study it with modern quantitative methods—hence we all suffer from shifting baselines. What we believe is normal is not necessarily natural; more likely, it's just the way the world was when we first saw it. This syndrome affects not only fisheries but all aspects of our life.

For example, the inhabitants of some large Asian cities wear masks outside home, especially when pollution levels rise above what's accepted as safe. Children born in Asia today may think that's normal, but 25 or 50 years ago, no one would have been seen wearing a mask.

My friend and colleague Jeremy Jackson helped reshift our baselines in the world of marine ecology with the publication of a seminal—and unexpected—paper titled "Reefs Since Columbus." I remember attending a presentation by Jeremy at a congress on marine conservation biology in 1997, at the University of Victoria in Canada. After having heard many other speakers in a day that was getting way too long, Jeremy walked with determination to a transparency projector mid-stage and started showing maps and data. His deep voice and original thinking captivated the audience. He woke us all up to the fact that the large animals in the ocean— whales, sea turtles, sharks—were once overwhelmingly more abundant than we, including scientists and fishermen, had ever thought. He used historical accounts to reveal a world of abundance at levels unimaginable. For instance, Andrés Bernáldez, writing about Columbus's second voyage, in 1494, wrote that the sea was so thick with sea turtles "that it seemed that the ships would run aground on them and were as if bathing in them." Jeremy carried out his presentation like a mad orchestra conductor, full of contagious energy. As we all listened, I'm sure we asked ourselves, What were we thinking? After his extraordinary performance, Jeremy whisked the last transparency off the projector and turned around, his long red ponytail waving. For a brief moment, you could hear a pin drop in the theater. And then, the audience—including many students—exploded in rapturous applause.

Loren McClenachan, a student of Jeremy's, later analyzed historical sources and estimated that back then there were up to 91 million adult green turtles in the Caribbean—some 300 times more than the current estimate of fewer than 300,000 green turtles there today.

HISTORY CAN RESHIFT our baselines. And protected areas, like the Medes Islands Marine Reserve, can help us too. What I saw at Medes over time was ecological succession in action: an ecosystem self-restoring and moving toward a more mature stage. That marine reserve was a window into the past.

I have seen the miracle of marine protected areas repeated all around the world. In 1999, Cabo Pulmo, in Mexico's Gulf of California, was close to being an underwater desert. My Mexican colleagues and I surveyed it as part of a larger diving study we conducted along Baja California. Back then, it was not different from the rest of the gulf—a shadow of its former glory after too much fishing—except that it had more corals than other areas. The fish populations were unremarkable. Four years earlier, though, the fishermen there, upset with not having enough fish to catch, did something that no one expected. Instead of spending more time at sea, trying to catch the few fish left, they stopped fishing—completely. They persuaded the Mexican government to create a national park in the sea—a no-take marine reserve. In four years not much had happened. But in 2009, my friend and former student Octavio Aburto returned to see how the Gulf of California was doing. He dived at all the places we had surveyed 10 years before. Cabo Pulmo served as our experimental locale, the place where fishing had stopped; elsewhere in the Gulf of California were control areas, where fishing had continued.

The control areas looked just as they had 10 years earlier, with unremarkable fish populations: just a handful of sharks, only occasional large groupers and snappers. And then came Cabo Pulmo. What had been a barren landscape a decade earlier was now a kaleidoscope of life and color. In a single dive one could see more sharks than our team had seen in the previous 10 years, along with spawning aggregations of large leopard groupers and Gulf groupers. We saw Cabo Pulmo come back to pristine in only 10 years, including the return of large predators—groupers, sharks, and jacks.

The return of the large predators inside marine reserves also creates trophic cascades, once their abundance recovers sufficiently. For example, in the Mediterranean and New Zealand, sea urchin predators (sea breams and snappers, respectively) reduce sea urchin density and consequently have shifted the ecosystem from a degraded, immature state (sea urchin barrens) to a complex, mature state (algal forests with high biodiversity). After five years of protection, the number of predators increases significantly. A full trophic cascade can take a decade or more.

Fully protected (no-take) areas where fishing is prohibited exhibit the largest positive changes and the fastest leaps along succession. A review of studies on 24 marine reserves in 29 countries showed that, on average, reserves contain 21 percent more species, and organisms are 28 percent larger than in unprotected areas nearby. My friend Sylvaine Giakoumi and I conducted a review of the literature, looking at the increased biomass of fish inside both fully protected areas and lightly protected areas where fishing is allowed. As shocking as it seems, most marine areas designated as "protected" permit fishing at different levels, from small levels of traditional fishing to industrial fishing including bottom trawling. Therefore we cannot put fully protected areas and lightly or minimally protected areas in the same bucket; it's apples and oranges, monkfish and octopuses. I had personally witnessed over 30 years of diving that lightly protected areas had fewer and smaller fish than no-take areas, and our analysis showed the same results: In protected areas that allow some fishing, the fish biomass does not even double. But in fully protected areas, the total biomass of fish is, on average, six times greater than in unprotected areas nearby, and sharks are 15 times more abundant. To allow fishing inside protected areas is to drop sand grains into the mechanism of the successional clock. The clock might be keep ticking for a while, but at some point it's going to clog and stop.

No one would be allowed to walk into the Louvre and pick any painting they fancy. Why should we allow people to remove endangered wildlife from areas that we deem so important that we should protect them? No conservationist would call a logging operation, no matter how well managed, part of a "protected forest," yet many self-identified conservationists and their organizations argue against fully protecting areas in the sea. Marine areas managed for responsible fishing are all good and necessary, but if we want to restore marine life in earnest and prevent the increasingly fast depletion of marine life and all the benefits it provides, we need to establish more no-take reserves. When I publish papers or give talks about marine reserves, I often hear from the usual suspects—both government officials and some fisheries scientists—that good fisheries management would make protected areas unnecessary. But fishing is the largest hunting operation left on the planet, targeting over half of the ocean surface, and no matter how restricted it may be, it continuously extracts wildlife from the ocean. How can that be a better tool for restoring biodiversity than protected areas where we let marine life fully bounce back and self-organize in complex ecosystems?

WHAT ABOUT THE LAND? Can national parks and other protected areas maintain and restore biodiversity in the way marine reserves do?

The answer reminds me of the saying, "Why do thieves rob banks? Because this is where the money is!" Nature tourists flock to national parks and nature reserves because that's where the animals are. Terrestrial protected areas are home to larger abundances of wildlife than unprotected areas. If you want to see wildebeests, lions, and zebras, the Serengeti National Park is a much better choice than areas in Kenya and Tanzania where wildlife is not protected. If you wish to see bison and wolves, visiting Yellowstone makes it easier than visiting an unprotected area in Wyoming.

Indeed, many studies show that terrestrial protected areas can protect habitats and species effectively. Species richness and animal abundance are higher inside protected areas than in unprotected areas nearby. As in marine reserves, so in terrestrial protected areas: Animals tend to be larger and wildlife biomass is proportionally larger than in nearby unprotected areas. In the tropics, protected areas have also been shown to be effective at reducing logging, hunting, grazing, and fires.

Protections don't just work because they were put into place; they require vigilant management. Illegal habitat conversion, hunting, and fishing conspire to deteriorate the health of the ecosystems they are meant to protect. But not only illegal activities degrade protected ecosystems: Governments can legally remove protections and reduce the size of protected areas. Once I thought that protected areas were sacred and untouchable—didn't we all?—but that's not true. Protected areas have been degazetted or reduced in size 700 times in the United States and Brazil's Amazonas State alone, with two-thirds of those changes occurring since the year 2000.

Breaking up or shrinking protected areas in the name of development is a doubly bad idea. First, all the gains accrued by protection can disappear swiftly. Second, size matters. For example, to fully protect the greater ecosystem, Yellowstone National Park would need to designate at minimum an area that encompasses the home range of the region's keystone species (the wolf) or its moving prey (the elk), whichever is larger. Anything smaller, and the wolves will venture out of the park boundaries in search of food. Outside the park, the conflict with ranchers becomes more likely, especially because the boundary between the park and surrounding ranches is quite sharp. Thus, the risk of wolves being shot increases, with all the consequences that come from a reduction in top predators.

In the Serengeti, a recent study showed that the pressure on ecosystems from outside, right up to the fence, makes wildebeests and other herbivores run from the park's edge, thus concentrating their grazing in the middle of the park. With their grazing impact concentrated in a smaller area, these animals are hampering the ability of the larger grassland to capture and store carbon. Perhaps the best example is the Amazonian forest, which, as we have seen, produces its own rain and weather patterns. Studies suggest that as of 2019, if as little as 15 to 20 percent of the forest cover were lost, the remaining forest would not be large enough to produce its own weather system, with catastrophic consequences for the entire planet.

So should all protected areas be large? When I started studying conservation biology in the 1980s, a debate was raging among academics: Is it better to protect one single large area or several small ones? It was called the SLOSS debate—single large or several small. Partisans of each current of thought arose, passionately defending their hypothesis and ignoring evidence that refuted it. Some questioned whether a small area alone was able to prevent extinction of a local population of plants or animals. Some insisted on the need to connect isolated protected areas by corridors so that the global population of threatened species would survive. But, long story short, we need both. Small protected areas may be the only practical tool in regions heavily populated by humans, and they may preserve species of insects or birds that are restricted to a single valley or small island. But for ecosystem benefits such as carbon storage and production of rain, the larger the protected area, the better.

AS WE CONSIDER the value of protected natural areas, the question always arises: What's in it for us humans? I have met a few fishermen who opposed the creation of even small marine reserves, afraid of conservationists wanting to prevent them from fishing. Maybe it had not been communicated properly to them, or maybe it's the classic reaction of blaming someone else for the depletion caused by oneself, but in any case, after a few years of protection, most of these fishermen are reaping the benefits of protection—and many of them are asking for exclusive access to the waters around the reserves, and even for expansion of the size of the reserves. Benefits to humans occur locally to globally, at sea and on land.

On land, mature forest ecosystems harbor not only the largest number of species but also huge amounts of carbon. The two are intimately connected. The large trees in old forests send carbon into the soil as they photosynthesize and store carbon in their wood. The protected forests that are still home to large fruit eaters, such as tapirs in South America and hornbills in Borneo, also store more carbon as these animals eat the fruit and disperse their seeds, their feces returning nutrients to the soil—good for the forest and for climate mitigation at the same time. Large herbivores in protected savannas—bison, buffaloes, and wildebeests, for example—enhance carbon sequestration in the soil because their grazing enhances plant growth and soil activity. At moderate levels, grazing actually keeps plants in a physiologically young stage for a longer time, thus stimulating the grass to continue growing.

Same for the ocean. Shark Bay in Australia is a large bay the size of the state of New Hampshire, its sandy bottom covered with large seagrass beds, which support large numbers of large herbivores—dugongs and sea turtles. Where there is prey, there are predators. Here, tiger sharks are the formidable predators that create a landscape of fear. The herbivores prefer the shallowest seagrass beds, less accessible to the large sharks. The deeper seagrass beds, where predation rates are higher, hold greater stocks of carbon. All told, these are healthy ecosystems, with complex food webs that result in significant carbon sequestration.

Protected areas restore the health of the ecosystem within, but what effect do they have on the health of humans? In 1982, Japan incorporated the practice of *shinrin-yoku,* which basically means hanging out in the forest, into the national health program. Some might make fun of tree huggers, using the term pejoratively, but we are learning that those whose life includes intimate moments in the forest might just be smarter and less stressed. And it's not just our imaginations, as it turns out. Trees emit oxygen as a by-product of photosynthesis, and they also secrete volatile oils that protect them from insects and pathogens. Turns out that these oils also help our immune system. As we breathe in, contemplative within the forest, our blood pressure goes down, and so does cortisol—the stress hormone.

It doesn't take a government-endorsed practice like shinrin-yoku for people to benefit from forests as therapy. Anyone in permanent contact with a protected area benefits significantly. A 2019 study compiled data on 87,000 children representing more than 60,000 households in 34 developing countries. Some lived near protected areas; others lived far from them. The authors found that households near protected areas that fostered ecotourism enjoyed 17 percent higher wealth levels and 16 percent less likelihood of living in poverty. Children under five living near these protected areas were 10 percent taller for their age and 13 percent less likely to be stunted than children living far from the forests. Interestingly, the study did not find any negative impacts on health because of living near protected areas. Research from 118 peer-reviewed articles likewise found those people living near older marine protected areas where no-take rules were well enforced also experienced positive well-being.

The value of protecting natural areas goes beyond our general well-being. Protected natural areas can save people's lives. In March 2019, Cyclone Idai devastated Mozambique. The rains created a biblical flood that killed more than a thousand people and destroyed thousands of homes. My friend Greg Carr, the hero behind the restoration of Mozambique's Gorongosa National Park, was closely involved in the disaster relief efforts. Park rangers were the first responders to arrive on the scene. Using satellite photographs in near real time, they identified flooded areas and safe routes for delivering food. Park staff provided emergency relief—including 220 metric tons of food and water—to nearly 40,000 people. The park itself lent survivors a huge hand. In nearby grasslands where livestock graze, the soil had been so degraded that it could not retain water, which slid over it as it does over asphalt. But the protected natural grasslands of Gorongosa absorbed rainwater equivalent to 800,000 Olympic swimming pools. Had that much water gone downstream, it could have created greater floods and loss of life.

Clearly protected areas can offer significant benefits not only for nature but also for people and their local economy. You would think we would make the most of this promise, but as I am writing these lines, only 7 percent of the ocean has been designated or proposed as protected, only 2.4 percent is fully protected from fishing, and only 15 percent of the land is protected. We need much more.

Recent reports indicate that humans have transformed—degraded—73 percent of the land. Forests have been so fragmented that, if we parachuted at any random point inside a forest anywhere in the world, there is a 70 percent chance that we'd be within one kilometer (3,200 ft) of the forest's edge. With only 27 percent of this planet we inhabit remaining as intact terrestrial ecosystems, it's just not enough: Not enough to prevent a mass extinction—up to one million species lost in the next decades, the United Nations predicts; not enough to prevent a 60 percent decline in terrestrial vertebrates since 1970, and the collapse of birds and insects around the world; not enough to support sufficient plants to absorb our excess carbon dioxide; not enough to help us mitigate the impacts of climate change. We need to keep what we have—conserving all the intact forests, grasslands, peatlands, wetlands, and other ecosystem types—and we need to do even better.

In the ocean, the main driver of biodiversity loss so far has not been habitat degradation but the extraction of biomass—fishing. (The one exception is on the continental shelves, where bottom trawling has been as destructive to ocean habitats as slash and burn practices have been to terrestrial.) But the patterns are the same. Currently 97 percent of the ocean is open to fishing of some kind. Protecting only 2.4 percent of the ocean has not been enough to prevent a 90 percent loss of large predatory fish such as sharks and tuna; not enough to halt the decline of coastal ecosystems.

NOT ENOUGH PROTECTION—that is the situation we see everywhere. Well, then, how much is enough? To make a difference for nature and for us, how much of the planet do we need to protect?

Scientific studies recommend that we safeguard half of the planet—land and sea—to preserve biodiversity and secure all nature's benefits upon which we depend, including carbon sequestration, so essential in helping us mitigate climate change—while managing our activities responsibly and sustainably in the other half. This conclusion coincides with survey results from around the world that show citizens wish that half the planet was protected.

It's an ambitious goal. It can be achieved if we expand the areas we protect to a total of 30 percent of the planet by 2030, designating another 20 percent "climate stabilization areas"—that is, ecosystems kept in a natural state so that they continue absorbing much of the carbon pollution that we expel into the atmosphere. Without that level of protection, it will be impossible to achieve the goal set by the 2015 Paris Climate Agreement.

Climate stabilization areas—also called carbon parks—may not be formally protected, but they already keep the forests and grasslands functioning. They include indigenous peoples' lands, which account for 37 percent of all remaining natural lands across Earth. These lands store almost 300 gigatons of carbon—about 30 times the world's global carbon emissions in 2019. Twenty percent of these lands lie within protected areas, but the rest remain natural thanks to the traditions of caring for the land. A sad example from 2019 comes from the Amazon, where tribes were forced to fight viciously to preserve their homelands and forests from cattle ranchers and miners, who are illegally cutting and burning the forest. Without indigenous peoples, the Amazonian rainforest would be much smaller than it is today. Their insights and voices are essential for keeping what healthy ecosystems we have left.

These indigenous peoples can remind us how far our baselines have shifted. Can we possibly find our way to protecting half the planet so our children's and grandchildren's baselines and notions of what a natural ecosystem looks like might return to those of centuries past? How can we make it happen in time? Is it enough to stop destructive human activities in protected areas and wait for ecosystems to self-restore? Or is there a way to accelerate ecological succession?

CHAPTER ELEVEN

REWILDING

CREATED IN 1872 by the United States government, Yellowstone was the first official national park in the world. It was protected because of its natural beauty and outstanding ecological value, yet no one questioned the killing of wolves that lived there. In Europe and North America, deep-seated fears have for centuries portrayed the wolf as *the* beast to exterminate. Wolves were seen as enemies—and still are by many—that killed livestock, game species like deer, and even people. Government policies cemented that belief, and wolves were systematically exterminated from many countries. We now know that wolves do not kill people—but, ironically, dogs kill 25,000 people globally every year because of rabies, yet nobody calls for the extermination of dogs. It seems as though we are happy with the domesticated version of the wolf, which we manipulated genetically over millennia, but we do not dare to look into the eyes of the wild wolf and try to understand who it is and what it does. But scientists now know that wolves hold the ecosystem together.

No one understood that in the decades after Yellowstone was established. Wolf extermination was the rule, and the last wolf was seen there in the 1920s. Fast-forward 70 years. In 1994, Yellowstone was a beautiful world of geysers and winter snowy landscapes, abundant with elk *(Cervus canadensis).* But those animals overgrazed the riverbanks. They were eating not only the grasses and underbrush but also the seedlings of cottonwood, aspen, and willow, which used to grow right down to the river's edge. Park managers tried to manage the elk population, as they put it, by culling them, but reducing their numbers did not reduce their impact.

Ecologists realized there might be a way for nature herself to restore the balance in Yellowstone, since human management was not working. The natural food web needed to be restored by reintroducing the top predator—the wolf. So in 1995, 31 wolves were released in Yellowstone, with the expectation that they would regulate the elk numbers better than humans had.

The plan worked. These 31 wolves and their descendants acted like landscape engineers and transformed the entire park. The wolves did reduce—and regulate—the number of elk, but they also changed the elk's behavior. By their presence alone, the wolves created a landscape of fear whereby elk spent less time in the open, to avoid being killed—just as the tiger sharks did in Australia's Shark Bay. Within a few years, the trees on the riverbanks were coming back. With more arboreal habitats, songbird populations increased. Forests of cottonwood, aspen, and willow now shaded and cooled the streams, reducing erosion and providing cover for fish and other aquatic life.

Thanks to the new riverside forests, the beaver population grew 12-fold in only 13 years. More beaver dams and richer habitats allowed otters, frogs, and reptiles to increase. Since the wolves hunted coyotes, coyote prey increased. With more rabbits, mice, and other small mammals throughout the park, the numbers of their predators—eagles and foxes, for example—multiplied.

But there is more. Before the reintroduction of the wolves, many elk died during severe winters and at the end of moderate winters, their winter mortality caused when food resources got buried in deep snow. Scavengers—ravens, eagles, foxes, bears, and coyotes—fed heavily on elk carcasses during these winter seasons. Global heating since 1948 has made the winters get shorter, though. Earlier snow thaws reduced late winter deer mortality, which meant less food for the scavengers. All that changed once wolves were reintroduced. Wolves preyed on elk, which made carrion available throughout even the warmer winters. More carrion meant more scavengers, helping to recycle the recent necrosphere, which nourished living matter once again.

In short, reintroducing wolves enriched Yellowstone's ecosystem and brought it closer to its mature state. The wolves—Yellowstone's top predator—are the hero of this story. The return of the wolves to Yellowstone caused the return of all creatures, plants and animals, from small to large, and it is also helping to buffer the impacts of global heating.

Wolves are the epitome of a keystone species. Their role in the terrestrial ecosystem is as provider of life for all types of creatures, in stark contrast to the demonic image that humans tend to project on them. Rewilding Yellowstone with the top predator helped rewind the successional clock and get the ecosystem moving forward toward more mature stages of the ecological succession. Without the wolves, the ecosystem was moving backward.

Top predators are the first to go when humans arrive to a place. We don't tolerate competition. We crave being the only ones at the top of the food web, sovereigns who prefer shorter and simpler food webs and small species with high turnover rates as our subjects. Our inclination has been either to keep ecosystems stuck or to force them to regress to earlier successional stages. Can we change that habit? Can we help ecosystems move beyond the roadblocks we have put in the way that keep them from maturing?

The answer is yes, through the process of rewilding. We were able to rewild Yellowstone, and look what happened. By rewilding, we reintroduce native species to restore the full natural cycle of an ecosystem. By reintroducing apex predators, like the wolves in Yellowstone, we can accelerate the restoration of ecosystems. But apex predators can only effect this trophic cascade if they slot back into an ecosystem with its full complement of prey species—that is, into wilderness areas or protected areas of a certain age. Could we do the same thing by reintroducing herbivores—species that eat plants and are prey to the apex predators? An example from the Serengeti will help answer that question.

A disease in Serengeti National Park provided a natural experiment at the scale of a large ecosystem, something that would be impractical through experimental manipulation. In 1890, within two years, a viral disease called rinderpest killed 95 percent of the wildebeests and buffaloes in East Africa. Passed on from livestock, rinderpest causes fever, diarrhea, inflammation of the mucous membranes, and high mortality. A treatment was established, and by 1963 all the livestock around the park had been vaccinated. When the disease disappeared in livestock, the wild animals bounced back: from 250,000 wildebeest in 1961 to 1.3 million in 1977. More wildebeests helped the Thomson's gazelles, which prefer to forage in places where wildebeests have already grazed. With more ungulates as prey, the populations of hyenas and lions also increased. In addition, more grazing wildebeests kept the grass short. Fewer plants grew old and withered, which meant the landscape contained less dead plant material and thus less fuel for wildfires. With fewer fires, more acacia tree seedlings survived. Giraffes love to eat acacia seedlings, and the renewed acacia abundance helped boost the giraffe numbers. More browsing giraffes meant fewer acacias grew into tall trees, but more young acacia shrubs sprouted, providing healthy underbrush and more organic debris into the system.

Another trophic cascade in reverse, from the bottom up—or, still better, across the food web. In this case, rewilding involved not reintroducing species but ensuring the health and proliferation of species in distress.

Rewilding not only accelerates ecological succession; it also can help mitigate climate change, as mature ecosystems sequester and store more carbon than degraded ecosystems. For example, many trees in tropical rainforests need large mammals to perpetuate their species. Tapirs in South America and elephants in West Africa, for example, eat the fleshy fruit from the trees and disperse the seeds that pass through the animals' digestive systems. Trees with large fruits tend to be taller and have denser wood, storing more carbon than other trees, which makes the larger mammals who can eat those fruit all the more important. Recent studies suggest that the loss of large fruit-eaters could lead to 12 percent carbon losses in tropical forests—another contributor to global warming. Rewilding our increasingly fragmented tropical forests with these large animals—or simply prohibiting the killing of them—would be beneficial to humanity and the rest of life on the planet.

YELLOWSTONE AND SERENGETI National Parks were protected areas that benefited from rewilding, whether intentional or unintentional. But could rewilding help restore other parts of the planet—even unprotected ecosystems? What about depleted farmland—the closest thing to zero biodiversity our planet has? Would it even be possible to re-create the natural ecosystem that was there before?

In 1987, Charlie Burrell inherited a British farm from his parents. This was not just any farm: It was Knepp, in West Sussex, a 1,400-hectare (3,500-acre) estate that dated back to the 12th century and had seen the visits of kings. By the 20th century, when Burrell got the farm, however, they couldn't turn a profit because they couldn't compete with farms on better soils. Both the fields and the dairy business were in ruins. The soil—in cross section, 320 meters (1,050 ft) of clay over a bedrock of limestone—was, according to Isabella Tree, Burrell's wife, "concrete in the summer and porridge in the winter." The arable fields had been plowed ad nauseam and subjected to artificial fertilizers, pesticides, and herbicides for a long time before they took over. Trying their best to make a profit, Burrell and Tree did as other farmers these days do: They started using fertilizers, pesticides, and fungicides, to try to make the farm more productive. They tried to diversify, they invested in infrastructure and new machinery, tried new varieties of crops, but after 12 years of hard work, they still failed to make a profit. With few options left, they sold their cows and equipment—whose proceeds cleared their debts—and stopped farming.

But they stayed with the land. They had some notion that perhaps they could restore its natural ecosystem. Repton Park, around the house, had been plowed up during World War II as part of the Dig for Victory campaign. Their first step was restoring it—a project for which they received Countryside Stewardship Scheme funding. With those funds they purchased Low Weald native wildflower seeds and began to sow them in the park. "That first year I remember walking out of the door through knee-high wildflowers, and hearing that incredible sound of insects," Tree said. "We hadn't known that that was what we'd been missing. And then of course the insects came back, and then the birds came back." Centuries of land degradation, plowing, and the intensive use of artificial fertilizer and pesticides after World War II had annihilated most life in the fields of England save the monoculture crops being grown there. People had almost forgotten that insects could be plentiful in the English countryside. "I remember in the 1970s, when I was a child growing up in Dorset, having to put the wipers on to wipe all the splatted insects off the windscreen," Tree told me. "That doesn't happen anywhere now—except in a very few areas, including Knepp."

But this was just the beginning of their rewilding experience. They heard about Frans Vera, a Dutch ecologist who hypothesized what Europe's lowlands must have been like when all the large herbivores roamed in abundance. Once there were the aurochs (wild cattle), the tarpans (wild horses), and the European bison—all depicted in prehistoric cave drawings. They were all long gone, except for the bison, which miraculously survived in captivity after the last animals in the wild were shot in the 1920s, and which are now being reintroduced in rewilding projects across Europe.

There were once other herbivores as well, such as red deer, moose, wild boar, and beavers by the many millions—and brown bears, too. We did not drive those extinct, although we overhunted moose, beavers, and bears. The vast numbers of these animals in the past must have had a significant influence on the structure of lowland European ecosystems.

The idea of rewilding Knepp with such creatures appealed to Burrell and Tree. Unable to bring back the old animals à la Jurassic Park, they found modern species that could mimic the role of the wild herbivores in the ecosystem—grazing animals that are, as Isabella put it, "proxies for the animals that would have been present in huge numbers in our landscape in the distant past." Thus, they introduced longhorn cattle for aurochs, Exmoor ponies for tarpans, Tamworth pigs for wild boars, and red and fallow deer. (Roe deer were already present in small numbers.) This suite of animals represented a combination of different eating preferences and habits. Diversity in action. We don't know how many species of plants the longhorn cattle feed on, but cattle in general can carry more than 230 seed species in their gut, their hooves, and their fur. So they eat here and poop there, and the seeds are given a jump start with the compost that surrounds them. The cattle don't eat thistles, but the ponies like them, and they also can stomach rougher grasses than cattle can. And the pigs rootle in search of roots, tubers, worms, and other invertebrates, aerating the soil.

"What we've done here is take our hands off the steering wheel, and just stand back and let nature take over," said Tree. And nature took over indeed. The new herbivores played such a diversity of ecosystem roles, replacing the uniform, depleted fields of the farm with a vastly superior mosaic of habitats, including water meadows, thorny scrub that protects young trees, sallow groves, and dead trees that provide a habitat for many animals. Nightingale territories on the farm increased threefold in a decade. The turtle dove, a species thought to be on its way to extinction in the British Isles, is increasing in numbers. The number of small skipper butterflies increased by 1,100 percent in just one year. The insects returned, and then the little birds came back to eat the insects, and then the predators returned. Now peregrine falcons nest at Knepp, and all five British owls are found there. The little owls are doing great. They eat the dung beetles found in cattle feces, but now the feces contain none of the pesticides or medicines omnipresent when the dairy farm was in operation. In the past, the pesticides and antibiotics given to the dairy herd ended up in their dung, killing any insect that encountered it.

Burrell and Tree let nature take charge and reestablish its wild ecosystem. The only thing they control is the number of herbivores, because they don't have any natural predators to prevent that population from increasing to the point of decimating the vegetation and starving themselves. The last wolf in England was apparently killed in 1390, and the last wolf in the British Isles was killed in Scotland in 1680.

So instead of relying on a top predator to keep the herbivores in check, which would be challenging to reintroduce in populated southern England, Burrell and Tree control the numbers of cattle, deer, and pigs that roam their farm, and they sell their meat—locally and by mail order. A conservation business.

If all those benefits weren't enough, Burrell and Tree started a safari business at Knepp, offering visitors what they call "microadventures." Tourists, especially bird-watchers (an abundant breed in Britain), can come to Knepp to observe what has been lost elsewhere. "This is a sustainable business," said Burrell. "The cash that comes through the safari business seems to be bigger and better than what it was when it was a commercial farm."

Not only the business but the entire landscape has been refreshed by rewilding—a transformation that has significant implications for the planet. The new diversity of vegetation and the restored soil retain water after heavy rains. The diverse plant communities of Knepp thus help reduce flooding and loss of infrastructure. More plant material and animal feces, together with abundant earthworms, dung beetles, and all the other invertebrates digesting the dung, added to the herbivore grazing and browsing that stimulates roots underground and vegetation regrowth aboveground. All combine to help build healthy soil, with its glomalin, that powerful carbon kidnapper specifically associated with mycorrhizal fungi. Mycorrhizal fungi has tripled in Knepp's soil since Burrell and Tree rewilded; soil biota and soil carbon have both doubled. Healthy soil rich with all that organic matter locks more carbon up, making the soil a great carbon sink again.

But Burrell and Tree did not return Knepp to its prehuman condition. Located near Gatwick Airport, Knepp is surrounded by roads. Its soils have been affected by nearly 70 years of chemical additives and hundreds of years of plowing. One generation's efforts cannot undo these influences completely. What we can do, however, is use our increasing knowledge of how pristine ecosystems perform to inform our decisions on how to restore today's ecosystems. We can use the tools available—the remaining megafauna, the principles of hydrology, plant and animal reintroductions—to create novel ecosystems: ecosystems with conditions and species that have never come together during our lifetimes, but which approach the successional maturity that makes them resilient in response to human impacts. It's not always a matter of returning to a prehuman ecosystem. The important thing is helping an ecosystem to function and mature. Therefore, rewilding is about the future—not the past.

Imagine if this sort of change could happen over and over around the planet. And if monoculture agriculture shifted to regenerative practices that help build the soil instead of damaging it, the change would create new potent carbon sinks, helping reduce global heating. A recent study suggested that mitigating agricultural practices could lower global temperatures as much as 25 percent of the 2°C (3.6°F) goal set by the Paris Climate Agreement.

WHILE REWILDING HAS proved effective in restoring lost ecological functions and accelerating ecological succession, we have to be careful about what species to reintroduce. Burrell and Tree were right in introducing species with ecosystem roles similar to those of the animals that roamed their land before humans. But not all species that look the same do the same. Let's go back to Yellowstone, but this time for an example of an ecosystem wrecked by introducing the wrong species.

President Theodore Roosevelt is an icon of American conservation. He created 150 national forests, 51 federal bird reserves, four national game preserves, five national parks, and 18 national monuments, representing more than 230 million acres of publicly protected land in the United States between 1901 and 1909. He also signed the Antiquities Act in 1906, which has allowed American presidents ever since to designate national monuments in order to protect sites of unique historical or natural importance. Ironically, despite his extraordinary record of protecting nature in the United States, Roosevelt was a big game hunter known to have bagged 296 wild animals, including 17 lions, during a single East Africa safari in 1909. His son Kermit killed 216 animals on the same trek.

As an avid hunter, Roosevelt held that the white man's recreational enjoyment of nature was more important than ecological health—or maybe he had simply not made the connection yet; few had. For the sake of enriching tourists' fishing experiences, he promoted stocking lakes in the West with game species. Perhaps well-intentioned, this philosophy came to harm Yellowstone National Park some 90 years later.

The only member of the trout family—the salmonids—native to Yellowstone Lake is the cutthroat trout. There were an estimated 3.5 million of them there in the 1970s, making them the dominant predatory fish in the lake. These trout live in shallow waters, eating mostly cladocerans—water fleas just a few millimeters long, but larger than most lake plankton. Cladocerans eat smaller crustaceans (copepods), and copepods eat algae, thus keeping the lake population of microscopic algae—phytoplankton—balanced and making the lake productive. The cutthroat trout is in turn eaten by otters, bears, bald eagles, and ospreys. During their spawning season, cutthroat trout migrate from the lake to its tributary streams, transporting nutrients as they do.

In 1994, the lake trout—not native to Yellowstone—was first observed in the lake. Sportfishermen had introduced the species illegally into a nearby lake in the 1980s, intending to improve game fishing in the area. It proved to be an example of the wrong type of rewilding, caused by the myopic belief in man's right to dominate nature.

As the lake trout population boomed, cutthroat numbers plummeted, declining by more than 90 percent by 2012. The game fish had become an invader—and a top predator, gobbling up the native trout. In 1998 alone, lake trout ate between three and four million cutthroat trout. The National Park Service quickly started a gillnetting program to rid Yellowstone Lake of the introduced species, and between 1998 and 2012, more than a million lake trout were removed from the lake. Yet that did not prevent the introduced species from increasing exponentially: from 125,000 adult fish in 1998 to 953,000 fish in 2012.

The introduction of lake trout and the decline of the cutthroat, the native top predator, caused trophic cascades within and outside of the lake. In the lake, without the cutthroat to eat them, the cladocerans increased in abundance and ate small copepods. Without small copepods, large copepods—too large to be eaten by cladocerans—boomed, and in turn ate more phytoplankton. With less phytoplankton, the primary productivity of the lake—the base of the food web—declined, affecting everything above. Since the lake trout lives in deeper water than the cutthroat, it is not accessible prey for bears, otters, and waterbirds including ospreys and eagles. All indicators showed these species declined. In 1997, 38 nesting ospreys lived at Yellowstone Lake; only three remained in 2017. In the late 1980s, grizzly bears caught more than 20,000 cutthroat trout in the spawning streams per year; by the late 2000s, that number had dropped to only 300. The abundance of river otters was the lowest ever estimated in 2008.

One new species added to the mix, strictly for human entertainment, caused a trophic cascade that reverberated through the entire Yellowstone Lake ecosystem, from microscopic phytoplankton to large mammals like otters and bears. Monumental efforts have been applied to reduce the abundance of lake trout in Yellowstone. In 2017, more than 9,200 kilometers (5,700 mi) of gillnets were set—the distance from New York to Cairo as the bird flies—during a grueling season lasting from May to September. Lake trout catches started to decline, and some experts believe we have reached a turning point. While full eradication of the lake trout is deemed impossible, continued efforts will likely reduce its population over time, and the local cutthroat trout will hopefully rebound. But we cannot drop our guard. The moral of this story: Rewild with care.

Rewilding with the right species—native herbivores or carnivores—at the right time can restore ecological functions that were lost—natural grazing or predation—and, under the right conditions, help an entire ecosystem self-restore. In a protected area where everything is missing except the keystone predator, its reintroduction can accelerate ecological succession and restore the complexity and maturity of the ecosystem. Even in a degraded area, like a moribund industrial farm, the right species can restart progress toward a healthy, productive, and ultimately mature ecosystem. The introduction of non-native species can on the other hand wreak havoc within an ecosystem. Inside a protected area, introducing the wrong species can actually reverse the gains accumulated by protection.

Rewilding

Our world has become less wild because we have trans-formed intact ecosystems into agricultural fields, grazing ranges, hunting and fishing destinations, and cities. Losing these wild places, we have lost most benefits they provide for us as well, such as flood protection, water security, water filtration, clean air, and naturally fertile soil. Rewilding the world could help us regain some of these benefits. But is utility for humans the most important way to measure the value of recovering the wild? Are there more powerful reasons why we should stop our assault on the natural world? Are there deeper reasons why we should do all we can to rewild wisely and protect and preserve the wild? In short, why and how should we value the natural world?

CHAPTER TWELVE

THE MORAL IMPERATIVE

HAVE YOU EVER stood in front of a painting at a museum, mesmerized by an unexpected quality that pulls you in—makes you smile, makes you cry, gives you the chills—but you can't explain why? Maybe it's the color palette, maybe it's the figures in the picture, maybe it's the ethereal atmosphere, maybe it's just the painting's energy. Do you need to understand what the picture is about to stand there, hypnotized and mouth agape? Have you experienced the same sense of awe and wonder amid a natural landscape? A sunflower field? A lake edged by evergreens? A cove surrounded by red rocks crowned by green pines?

As a scientist, I have spent decades collecting and analyzing data, turning ecosystem structure and dynamics into numbers and graphs, trying to embroider the baroque complexity of nature onto one neat pillowcase, modeled by just a few equations. But I also know that I loved the natural world before I could understand it. In fact, I was interested in understanding it *because* I loved it. And now, the more I know intellectually about the natural world, the more I realize how little I know—and yet my love grows deeper.

There is something very deep in our souls, an innate attraction between us humans and the natural world that sends us seeking unfiltered contact with nature and with the other forms of life that share this planet. My colleague and hero Ed Wilson calls it "biophilia"—from the Greek for "love of life"—which he defines as "the urge to affiliate with other forms of life." Whatever it is, every child feels it every day, several times a day. Just watch children left alone to explore a grassy meadow full of wildflowers and butterflies, or mesmerized by a galaxy of fireflies in a forest, or watching crabs scuttling around in a tide pool. That little child's wonder is in us all.

Why do we care about protecting other creatures? Do we just want to save that memory of our childhood? Is it empathy for fellow living beings? Once we are adults, is it still love, or is it a moral obligation?

Let's consider the moral dimensions of conservation. What do world religions say about this? All holy books are open to interpretation, but there seems to be a common theme. All religions make it clear that we should not destroy God's creation. In Jewish tradition, God owns the land and the environment, and humans have a duty to take care of them: "The land shall not be sold in perpetuity, for the land is mine; with me you are but aliens and tenants" (Leviticus 25:23). Buddhist teachings communicate the value of conservation over environmental destruction: "As a bee—without harming the blossom, its color, its fragrance—takes its nectar and flies away: so should the sage go through a village" (Dhammapada IV, Pupphavagga: Blossoms, 49). The Shinto religion is based on a belief in spirits linked to natural entities such as water, rocks, and wind. Forests are sacred. Shinto followers are expected to live in harmony and peaceful coexistence with both other human beings and nature. In Islam, wasteful consumption (Isrāf) is the 32nd greatest sin. The Quran dedicates hundreds of verses to caring for the environment, saying we should "not strut arrogantly on the earth. You will never split the earth apart nor will you ever rival the mountains' stature" (Quran, Sura XVII: 37). God's creation is inviolate, and we are entrusted to preserve it.

The message of Christianity is mixed. Surely the world is seen as God's creation and hence worthy of care, but some passages in the Book of Genesis suggest that man, made in God's image, has dominion over Earth. The man-as-master message of the Christian Bible may have arisen because of textual ambiguities or utilitarian and self-serving interpretations, and recent Christian messages have emphasized conservation and the moral edict of care for, not dominion over, God's creation. Pope Francis has been particularly influential with his second encyclical letter, "Laudato si'," published in 2015 ahead of the historic Climate Change Conference in Paris. Pope Francis wrote: "Although it is true that we Christians have at times incorrectly interpreted the Scriptures, nowadays we must forcefully reject the notion that our being created in God's image and given dominion over the earth justifies absolute domination over other creatures." According to Francis, the Bible tells us that each creature has its own purpose, that "none is superfluous." The material universe speaks of God's boundless affection for us, Francis also wrote: "Soil, water, mountains: everything is, as it were, a caress of God." Therefore, wanton destruction of the material universe is a sin and a rejection of God's love.

My friend Carl Safina put it beautifully: "No religion has ever preached that our role on earth is to destroy, or to leave less for those who'll come after us. No wisdom tradition teaches that it's O.K. for a generation to drive the world toward ruin. We are taught instead that we must safely pilot the ark." In other words, religions all tell us we should care for creation.

ALTHOUGH SOME ANCIENT SOCIETIES, such as the Maya and Easter Islanders, collapsed partly because of their overuse of the natural world around them, most indigenous groups have lived sustainably in their environment for millennia. Most see themselves as part of nature, not masters of it. Some ask for forgiveness as part of the act of killing a fellow Earthling for food. Many view natural formations—mountains, springs, or rivers, for example—as sacred.

A recent court case in New Zealand caught the world's attention. In 2017, Maori tribes on the North Island won legal recognition of the Whanganui River as an ancestor, holding the same rights as a person. "We can trace our genealogy to the origins of the universe," Gerrard Albert, a Maori leader in the region, said. "And therefore rather than us being masters of the natural world, we are part of it. We want to live like that as our starting point." Soon after, two more legal actions followed this precedent as the New Zealand Parliament granted similar rights to a 2,100-square-kilometer (820 sq mi) region, a former national park called Te Urewera, and a mountain.

Ecological science shows us that ecosystems are composed of an interacting community of creatures and the landscapes in which they live. Every creature has a different role, but the ecosystem is the combination of all the creatures within and the interaction dynamics among them. There would be no whole without the parts. Therefore, all creatures have intrinsic value because they belong to the constitution of our biosphere.

That may be a way of stating the value of nature based on science, but I believe that deep and inexpressible love of nature—biophilia—is more powerful than any rational construct as an answer to the question of why we should care for the natural world.

LOVE IS what our National Geographic Pristine Seas team has used to inspire leaders to protect some of the wildest places in the ocean. Here is the story of how we did it.

In academia we were taught to be rational, to let our brains dominate our feelings and values. We assumed that people would make the right decision if they had all the available information. We published our research in peer-reviewed journals. That was our job. I expected politicians to be aware of our research results and act accordingly. I was trapped in the ivory tower, self-contented, with the academic illusion that it was other people who were supposed to understand the implications of our research and take action in the real world. Why should I go the extra mile and explain our research, what it meant, and why it was important—let alone do anything about it?

Little did I know how wrong I was.

Luckily, I was taught and mentored by ecologists who believed that the study of natural history is more poetry than engineering, and by communicators who taught me why to make my research relevant to society and how to communicate that to key audiences. I put that learning into action as we developed Pristine Seas. Once I joined the National Geographic Society, I learned the secret to inspiring leaders to commit to protecting natural places: Let them fall in love with those places.

In October 2012, we conducted a Pristine Seas expedition to the shores of Gabon, a country in West Africa with more than 80 percent of its terrestrial surface covered in rainforests, and long uninhabited shores where endangered sea turtles nest and hippos surf in the Atlantic Ocean waves. We had been invited by Lee White, then the director of Gabon's National Parks Agency, and Mike Fay, a fellow National Geographic explorer who walked 2,000 miles in 1999 across the wildest tracts of forest in West Africa, from Congo to the beaches of Gabon. His epic trek, called the Megatransect, resulted in the creation of 13 national parks in Gabon. We explored the waters along the coast of Gabon, spending three weeks aboard the expedition vessel *Plan B*, provided for the project by my dear friend Ted Waitt, chairman of the Waitt Foundation. We dived off beaches in water so murky that we could not see our fins. We scouted out shipwrecks giving shelter to goliath groupers six feet long. We plunged under oil platforms rich in schools of large fish such as tuna and jacks, hearing as we did the mesmerizing songs of the humpback whales underwater. Lee and Mike finally persuaded Gabon's President Ali Bongo Ondimba to come aboard and learn what we had found. He joined us on the last day of the expedition, when *Plan B* was anchored in water more than 100 meters (330 ft) deep on an offshore seamount at the northern edge of the country's marine territory.

I made a presentation including photographs and short video clips. President Bongo Ondimba watched attentively and talked with us a bit more, but after about an hour, I saw him look at his watch. I thought we were going to lose him. Then we invited him to pilot *Plan B*'s remotely operated vehicle (ROV)—a submersible robot tethered to the ship and armed with a camera that allows one to watch the underwater world in real time. That raised his interest level again, and so he sat at the ROV console, watching the screen as he drove the ROV as if he was playing a video game. The sub reached the bottom, 100 meters down, on top of the flat seamount. Sand. And more sand. There was nothing exciting to see—and now we were going to lose him for sure, I feared.

But then he shifted direction and moved the ROV toward the edge of the seamount. A dark shape appeared in the distance. As the camera drew closer, the shape materialized: a dark rock full of holes and crevices, home to thousands of brittle stars covering the rock, moving their arms and trying to capture food from the water. We saw dozens of scorpionfish a foot long, with red and white patches and erect dorsal spines, lying on the seafloor. Hundreds of bright orange anthias, colorful little fish with long pectoral fins, hovered above the scorpionfish. We were all glued to the screen. We asked the president to let the ROV settle on the sand so we could all just enjoy the spectacle. It took only a minute for a big head with round eyes to loom into view, coming closer and closer, checking out its own reflection in the domed camera lens. It was a dogtooth grouper with a gray body the size of a bicycle, that distinctive frowning mouth, and three dark stripes radiating back from each eye. The grouper just hovered in front of the camera. And then another showed up, and another. Finally, five huge dogtooth groupers were staring into the camera, frozen as if caught in the headlights. And so were we. I looked at the president, and I could feel that he had just fallen in love with the underwater world of his own country—a natural wonderland that he did not really know.

The plan worked. On his way back to Libreville, the capital, President Bongo Ondimba told Mike and Lee that now he understood he had to protect these waters. He went on to create a network of marine protected areas that not only preserve Gabon's unique marine biodiversity but also act as engines to replenish surrounding local fisheries. That network comprises 20 marine protected areas now covering 46,000 square kilometers (17,760 sq mi)—28 percent of Gabon's marine waters. It was a first for Africa, and an example seldom seen around the world.

This story from Gabon is typical for Pristine Seas. When we first meet with country leaders, we make sure we never get into the brainy weeds. We never show them data or refer to scholarly debates in academic journals, splitting hairs to the infinitesimal degree. We never start with the head. We go straight to the heart, and taking a leader to the field is the best recipe for doing so. We've taken heads of government and environment ministers diving with schools of thousands of silvery jacks. We've taken them down in a submarine to let them explore the twilight zone a thousand feet deep. They all come out smiling, like children in love with nature. When their busy schedules cannot accommodate a field trip, we bring these places to them. A 360-degree video headset allowed the president of Ecuador to experience a virtual dive among a school of hammerhead sharks. Even a two-minute video shown on my tablet to Ségolène Royal, the French minister of the environment, made her fall in love with a tiny coral atoll that France owns in the eastern tropical Pacific—and decide to protect it.

It is that sense of awe and wonder that makes people fall in love with the natural world and begin to care in ways they may never have known possible. Only when we have offered that experience to these key decision-makers do we bring in the scientific studies and economic analyses showing why these places need to be protected. Ultimately, these leaders will need the facts to explain the benefits of conservation over the status quo and reassure the minister of finance or fisheries that protecting pieces of the ocean makes sense. But always the love and fascination come first. Once they have fallen in love with nature, these leaders intuitively feel the responsibility to protect these places. They understand that it is their moral imperative.

WHAT IS THE VALUE of all creatures on Earth—bacteria, archaea, yeasts, fungi, sponges, jellyfish, diatoms, cladocerans, copepods, brachiopods, corals, snails, clams, ctenophores, cephalopods, sea squirts, nematodes, kinorhynchs, beetles, flies, bees, butterflies, spiders, worms, ungulates, lobsters, chaetognaths, shrimp, tortoises, sea urchins, crocodiles, sea cucumbers, crinoids, crabs, snakes, sipunculids, sea stars, sea turtles, birds, reptiles, fish, frogs, salamanders, mammals, algae, ferns, flowering plants— and the ecosystems they form? Age-old beliefs in the value of biodiversity based on its intrinsic value have lost strength as the conversation has shifted to instrumental value. Not only those concerned with the industrial economy but even ecologists themselves have tended to focus their arguments on the goods and services provided by ecosystems as they urge environmental management and decision-making. I have often had to plead guilty myself. When it comes to the natural world, can awe and wonder and love prevail over economics?

The fact is, though, even a coldhearted economic argument can be made in favor of preserving the wild.

CHAPTER THIRTEEN

THE ECONOMICS OF NATURE

IN APRIL 2018, I assembled a dream team of top
scientists and economists at the National Geographic Society in Washington, D.C. Our goal was to
prioritize what areas need to be protected in the
ocean, now and in the future. Previous efforts to
identify global conservation priorities had emphasized
biodiversity but ignored other uses we might make of the
ocean, such as tourism, fishing, or oil drilling, which gave
the impression that the decision had to be a win-lose situation, a trade-off between production—that is, extraction
of natural resources—and protection. In other words, the
unspoken assumption has been that protecting an area
from extractive activities will result in irreparable economic loss. This meant most efforts to identify conservation priorities remained academic exercises, and their

recommendations were seldom implemented in the real world.

We had to find a way to conserve ocean biodiversity while achieving other objectives, to respond to the major challenges to human society. But before we started, we needed to know how to break the perceived wall between production and protection. We needed to understand why extractive and destructive uses prevail in a policy world prioritizing economic growth, and we needed to test the traditional economic assumptions about biodiversity held by decision-makers.

For the last decade, my colleagues and I have met with presidents, prime ministers, and ministers of the environment to persuade them to protect some of the most wonderful places in the ocean. Almost inevitably, the conversation will come around to two questions: What about the fisheries? Won't a protected area destroy their business? It's the opportunity cost that scares these decision-makers, regardless of the future sustainability of their current activities. That's the main reason why we don't have more protected areas: Not because there is no scientific justification and not because there is no public demand for them, but because there is a perceived cost that will be felt by economically important extractive activities, whether it's logging in a forest, agriculture in the plains, or fishing at sea. Industry lobbies have a set playbook that they have been using successfully over time, scaring governments about the cataclysmic economic impact of protecting more of the natural world.

A classic case of such hyperbole occurred in 2017 when we asked the Mexican government to protect an area of 150,000 square kilometers (57,915 sq mi) in the Pacific around the Revillagigedo archipelago south of Baja California. Representatives of Mexico's tuna fishing industry claimed they catch most of their tuna in that area, and that establishing protections would sink their business and put thousands of families out of work. Furthermore, they argued, it would cause a decline in the tuna supply, which would raise the price of a can of tuna and cause public riots. The Mexican government could never agree to that.

We had heard this type of baseless exaggeration before. But we had facts to counter their claims. First of all, tuna are migratory species. They swim long distances throughout the year, so those not caught around the Revillagigedo Islands could be caught elsewhere. Furthermore, satellite data from transponders required on all tuna fishing vessels showed that the Mexican fleet caught less than 4 percent of its tuna in the area. In fact, the data showed that three-quarters of their catch came from international waters, beyond Mexico's jurisdiction. So we were able to call them on their lies, and then we went on to show them, using the findings I have shared in this book, that the reserve would benefit marine biodiversity and not affect their bottom line. Because it is always about the bottom line. In my experience, there is a 95 percent probability that the first question a finance minister will ask when discussing creating a protected area is, "How much is this going to cost?"

There is a clear moral argument for protecting more of the natural world. There is an even stronger human survival argument, because the loss of all ecosystem services would mean global human extinction. Thus, the value of the natural world must be infinite. Yet the traditional economic argument, win-lose in its assumptions, is prevalent in policymaking today. One reason is that political cycles are much shorter than ecological cycles. Because the first law of politics is to be reelected, short-term gain typically trumps long-term benefits. "Shareholder value" is the mantra of public corporations, in particular those driving decisions affecting the ecological and climate crisis, and those assessments are also short term. Quarterly financial returns for companies and investors, annual GDP growth for countries: Those are our modern golden idols. Everything else, including our well-being, is subservient to them. A finance minister tends to think about the opportunity costs of conservation—the forgone fishing or logging profits—plus the management costs of a protected area, which all add up to a resource sink that has to be funded by the government.

But might not the benefits of protection offset those costs?

MANGROVES ARE AMAZING TREES. They have developed the unique ability to live in seawater, and they fringe many of the tropical coasts around the world. In their natural state, mangroves develop a complex system of roots, a labyrinth that provides shelter for many species of fish and habitat for many other species, including oysters that are consumed by humans. My colleague Octavio Aburto did his Ph.D. thesis at the Scripps Institution of Oceanography under my supervision on this very ecosystem—the mangrove forests in Mexico's Gulf of California—and his work resulted in some fascinating economic discoveries.

The shores of Baja California are a desert, punctuated by small green mangrove patches. Swimming in those mangroves during the late 1990s, we realized that their intricate mesh of roots provided the main habitat for juvenile snappers. Ultimately, Octavio's work showed that snappers spend the first year of their lives in the mangroves. Once they achieve a size that gives them protection from most predators, they migrate out to adult feeding and reproductive grounds in the rocky shores nearby, where they may be caught by fishermen. Octavio spent many months visiting all mangroves along the peninsula, counting and measuring snappers and estimating the distances they travel after they leave the mangroves. He also measured the abundance of adult snappers caught by local fishermen at increasing distances from the mangrove forests, correlating abundance with distance. His results showed that every hectare (2.5 acres) of mangrove forest produced catchable fish with a median economic value of $37,500 per year. In contrast, the Mexican National Forest Commission had determined in 2006 that destroying one hectare of mangrove to develop or build shrimp farms had a cost of only $1,020 per hectare. Who knows who in the Mexican government decided that mangroves were worth so little, but they were clearly unaware of the value of the mangroves as a fish nursery, and they missed Octavio's estimate by 30 times.

But support of the fishing industry is just one ecosystem service provided by the mangroves. Mangrove forests capture a lot of sediment. In fact, they sequester 10 times more carbon per hectare than tropical forests do, and thus serve as a powerful engine for mitigating climate change. They also provide protection against destructive tropical cyclone waves: During the devastating 2004 Asian tsunami, the areas behind mangrove forests sustained less damage than those where the mangroves had been cut. And there may be ecosystem benefits from the mangroves that we have not even yet recognized. But for those who don't know, mangroves may just be a hotbed of mosquitoes and something to be destroyed in the name of coastal development.

Shrimp farms are one of the main drivers of mangrove loss in Southeast Asia. Mangrove forests are clear-cut, and the soil is excavated to create ponds ranging between the size of a football field and one square kilometer (0.4 sq mi), which are then filled with seawater. But current shrimp farming practices turn the ponds too saline and toxic in only five years, a time element that must be factored into the economic equation. Economists consider "net present value"—the current value of all future cash flows generated by a project, taking into account the risk of the investment and assuming that a dollar received today can be invested and earn interest, so it should be more valuable than the same dollar received years from now. The net present value of the operating returns over the five-year life span of a shrimp farm in southern Thailand is around $8,000 per hectare (2.5 acres), but factor in the cost of the water pollution it generates, and the total drops to only $200. In contrast, every hectare of intact mangrove forest in Thailand is worth $194,000 thanks to its many ecosystem services, including carbon sequestration, erosion control, protection from storms, food production, and recreation. Protecting the mangroves—and restoring lost ones—can generate far more economic value than converting them for shrimp.

IF A FINANCE MINISTER had all of this information, what would be the choice, to let the shrimp farming industry cut the mangroves or to support their protection? From an economic perspective, protecting the mangroves is a no-brainer. But it is always harder to make the argument that banning the extraction of wildlife from certain areas also has economic benefits.

In the late 1990s, I dived at the Columbretes Islands Marine Reserve off the Mediterranean coast of Spain, about 320 kilometers (200 mi) southwest of the Medes Islands. The Columbretes are the summits of old underwater volcanoes, and

5,543 hectares (21.4 sq mi) around them have been protected from fishing and other extractive activities since 1990. Rough and isolated, 50 kilometers (31 mi) offshore, the reserve there is enforced 24/7 by rangers stationed on the largest island. What struck me the most while diving there was the size of the spiny lobsters. They were monsters, compared with any others I had seen in the Mediterranean. In the decade between 1997 and 2007, some colleagues of mine tagged lobsters inside the reserve and found that 4 percent of the females and 7 percent of the males migrated outside of the reserve every year, becoming available to commercial fishermen. While the number of lobsters spilling over annually did not quite make up for the number lost when the reserve was established and fishing grounds were closed, the size of the lobsters emigrating from the reserve made up for the difference. The fishers now catch 10 percent more lobsters by weight around the reserve than they would if there were no reserve. Clearly the benefits of protection exceeded the opportunity costs.

Around the world, we can cite the same type of benefits gained by establishing marine reserves. In St. Lucia in the Caribbean, a small network of marine reserves was established that represented the closure of 35 percent of the island's fishing grounds, yet in only five years fish catches around the reserves increased between 46 and 90 percent. In Fiji's Ucunivanua Marine Reserve, clams became seven times more abundant in adjacent unprotected areas after only five years, thanks to the abundance of clam larvae produced inside the reserve. Off the Sinai Peninsula in Egypt, catch per unit effort increased by 66 percent around marine reserves within five years of protection. In Kenya's Mombasa Marine National Park, a typical fisherman's income near the no-take area was 135 percent higher than in open access areas far from the reserve. And so on and so forth. Again and again, the examples contradict the assumptions that protection will cost too much and show the long-lasting economic benefits of preserving marine areas.

TOURISM CAN BE another economic boost provided by protected areas, if well regulated. In October 2016, my partner, Kristin Rechberger, and I were sitting in a meadow carpeted with wet giant ferns in Volcanoes National Park in Rwanda. These volcanoes form a mountain chain that extends across the borders of the Democratic Republic of the Congo, Rwanda, and Uganda. This tri-national park and a separate patch of intact, protected forest in Uganda—the Bwindi Impenetrable Forest—harbor about 1,000 mountain gorillas, the last of their kind. About 600 of those gorillas live on the Rwandan side of the mountains. Below us stretched a stone wall, delimiting the national park in Rwandan territory—tall enough to prevent buffaloes from visiting cornfields outside the park, and impermeable enough to prevent agriculture from encroaching on the forest. Beyond the wall there is forest no more, but a sea of rolling hills covered by a quilt of small farms.

That sharp boundary is maintained by a subsidy of energy in the form of foreign currency from foreign tourists who come to see the gorillas. It takes money and human resources to keep the park protected, but it works for both gorillas and people. The 600 mountain gorillas in Rwandan territory bring over $200 million per year into the country, some of which is reinvested in the villages around the park. In fact, every mountain gorilla brings more wealth to Rwanda than the average businessperson in the country. The national park is the largest single source of employment and economic revenue in the province. But it's not only about the money: The intact forest protected by the park provides water security and stability, retaining rain in its soil and releasing water into the surrounding region steadily over time.

Ocean ecotourism can also generate extraordinary value. The Medes Islands Marine Reserve, where I did my early fieldwork, protects a very small no-take area—about one square kilometer (0.4 sq mi)—but it is home to an immense biomass of fish, one of the largest in the Mediterranean. The regional Catalan government created the reserve in 1983, after a long decision-making process and general opposition from both commercial and recreational fishermen. Management of the reserve was calculated to cost half a million euros per year, covered by government funds, and therefore the reserve was perceived as a sink of public resources. But after protection, the fish came back in earnest—quickly. And when the fish came back, the divers came in, from all over Europe. The reserve now supports an ecotourism operation that brings 12 million euros to the local economy annually, mainly through diving, snorkeling, and glass-bottom boats. The reserve value exceeded the pre-reserve value in only five years. Without the reserve, the net present value of the area for fishermen was 1.8 million euros over an eight-year period. Thanks to the current protections, net present value is eight million euros, because of increased tourism inside the reserve and better fishing around it—plus an additional several hundred jobs.

I have seen similar examples all around the world, including Cabo Pulmo, where the spectacular recovery of marine life after protection and the consequent development of well-regulated diving tourism made the local community wealthier than most other coastal communities in Mexico. On a larger scale, the Great Barrier Reef Marine Park—a 344,000-square-kilometer (132,819 sq mi) marine protected area, of which a third is fully protected from fishing—brought in 5.5 billion Australian dollars to the Australian economy and supported 54,000 jobs in 2007 through ecotourism, 36 times the revenue gained from commercial fishing. A similar story can be told about the national parks in the United States. While we may not have numbers to compare from before their establishment, we can certainly quantify their value today. In Yellowstone, the project to reintroduce the wolf has cost about $30 million, but wolf ecotourism brings in $35 million annually, providing an economic boom for the local communities around the park.

In 2018, 318,000,000 visitors spent an estimated $20 billion while visiting National Park Service lands, supporting 329,000 jobs, and producing a total value of goods and services of $40 billion. Every dollar invested by the federal government in management of our national parks generates $10 in economic output. Protecting the wild in places where people can come and delight in nature pays off.

AMID THIS INCREASING BODY of quantitative evidence on the economic benefits of protecting natural ecosystems, the status quo still favors exploitation over conservation. Despite lip service to sustainability, people and companies continue cutting down tropical forests at a rate equivalent to several football fields per minute, and industrial fishing vessels continue depleting fish populations globally. A major problem is the focus on maximizing the benefit from a single use of an ecosystem (timber or seafood, for example), which means destroying the ability of that ecosystem to provide any other benefits.

Let's examine an example from China. In the summer of 1998, it rained heavily there. For 60 days, water surged over the Yangtze River's banks, destroying everything in its path and causing some of the worst floods in modern Chinese history. Afterward, local leaders set out to understand why the floods had been so destructive. Everybody could remember worse storms, but none had done so much damage. It did not take them long to realize what had happened. In the years leading up to the flood, economic growth had come to the country, causing development that disrupted the balance between people and nature.

To meet the needs of a growing nation, upstream timber forests had been cut down and grasslands had been heavily grazed by livestock—changes that diminished the ability of these ecosystems to absorb the excess water. Without the trees dampening the rainfall and without healthy soil and natural grasslands retaining water, the rain just slid over the hardened ground. And, last insurance against flooding, the wetlands were gone because, to meet the increased need for housing, people had built over them. In large part because of the loss of these ecosystems, the 1998 floods caused $20 billion in damage and 3,600 lives were lost. After the tragedy, Chinese authorities recruited experts to try to restore those lost ecosystems. It would have been so much less costly in terms of money and human life to keep that green infrastructure in place to start with. Forests, grasslands, and wetlands had been their natural insurance against flooding.

The Yangtze flood is just one of many examples of how the natural world provides more benefits to us than just the market price of one commodity. Another example is food. Three out of four of the world's food crops depend at least in part on pollination by wild bees, butterflies, moths, wasps, beetles, birds, bats, and other vertebrates. The annual value of crops pollinated by animals globally ranges between

$235 billion and $577 billion. In the past 50 years, the volume of crops that depend on animal pollination has increased threefold, a value that can only continue increasing as the human population grows. Pollinators pollinate not only our food but also almost nine out of 10 wild flowering plants—which, as members of larger ecosystems, provide other benefits not captured here. But massive pesticide use worldwide is causing a worldwide decline in insect numbers. Ironically, our chosen way to prevent bugs from ruining our monoculture crops is annihilating the biodiversity that the crops depend on. We're killing the goose with the golden eggs.

IT HAS BEEN ESTIMATED that every year, the environment—our natural capital—provides $125 trillion in free support to human society and the global economy. That's almost twice the global GDP in 2011, when these estimates were obtained. Yet these are underestimates of the natural capital, because some ecosystem services were not included. Take oxygen, a gas that is essential for our survival—so essential that high-altitude climbers, when they reach the thin, oxygen-poor air above 8,000 meters (26,247 ft), call it the "death zone." The oxygen in the atmosphere is produced by bacteria and algae in the ocean and by the plants on the land. If we lost all these creatures that give us oxygen for free, could we replace their role? The replacement value is a common way for economists to determine the value of things. How much would it cost to produce all the oxygen in the atmosphere? Based on current costs, and assuming we had the industrial capacity, the price tag would be $186,000 trillion. (For those who like to see the numbers, $155 was the 2019 cost of extracting one metric ton of pure oxygen from air, and there are 1.2×10^{15} metric tons of oxygen in the atmosphere.) That means the value of the pure, free oxygen in our atmosphere is over 2,000 times the 2019 global GDP.

There's bad and good news. The bad news is that our overuse of the natural world, in addition to crippling our life-support system, is costing us seven trillion dollars every year. By 2050, those costs could rise to $28 trillion. The good news is that protecting our ecosystems can generate more value than if we were to convert them to agricultural monocultures or exploit them to the limit. Supporting a system of well-managed protected areas over a third of our planet, land and sea, could cost between $103 billion and $171 billion a year. The economic benefits would outweigh the costs; GDP would rise. That's a cheap investment to maintain a $125 trillion life-support system! But some people—including finance ministers—will still say that this is impossible, that it's too expensive and we don't have the money.

Do you know how much governments are spending to subsidize primarily industrial fishing and practices that perpetuate overfishing? Thirty-five billion dollars every year. And to subsidize industrial agriculture—the main driver of terrestrial biodiversity loss? Seven hundred billion dollars every year (but only one percent of that goes to activities that benefit the environment). And to subsidize the use of fossil fuel? The International Monetary Fund in Washington, D.C., estimated in 2015 that governments give away $300 billion pretax directly to the fossil fuel companies, and society pays for the costs of the impacts of burning fossil fuels—including traffic congestion, accidents, road damage, premature mortality from air pollution, forgone consumption tax revenue, and global warming—with a shocking five trillion dollars . . . *every year.* The money is there; it's just being used to buttress the very activities that are destroying our life-support system—and to perpetuate the same economic system that some "very serious people" are trying to protect.

ARMED WITH all of the above evidence, our team gathered at the National Geographic Society in April 2018 decided that in order to prioritize what areas in the ocean need protection, we had to develop a new framework with multiple objectives: not only conservation of ocean biodiversity but also provision of food for a growing human population and mitigation of the impacts of climate change. Our team worked for a year and a half, compiling databases from multiple sources to produce maps of the global ocean divided into pixels that we could rank in order of priority. Every pixel was approximately 50 by 50 kilometers (31 by 31 mi), giving us a database with more than 130,000 pixels. We compiled data on the geographic distribution, extinction risk, evolutionary uniqueness, and ecological role of each one of more than 6,000 species of plants and animals. We compiled maps of the main types of ecosystems in the ocean, from shallow to deep. We used estimates of the catch of every species per pixel, and generated a global map of carbon stocks in the first meter of the sediment on the seafloor, among other data. The computing power needed to analyze all of these data was so massive that Google agreed to provide up to 200 computers located in different places to run our analysis—a pro bono virtual supercomputer. Our ultimate goal: to come up with the amount of ocean needed to make a global difference—and we did.

Our results showed that a substantial increase in ocean protection could achieve triple wins, not only protecting biodiversity but also boosting fisheries productivity and securing marine carbon stocks to avoid additional greenhouse gas emissions. Specifically, by strategically protecting 35 percent of the ocean, we could preserve two-thirds of all possible benefits from biodiversity while increasing the global catch of fish by 9 million metric tons. (That's 91 percent of the potential maximum food provisioning secured by increased protection.) In other words, the amount of fish that would be restored and spill over the boundaries of these no-take marine reserves would exceed the opportunity costs (the value of the catch forgone because of these reserves).

We also found that bottom trawling is releasing carbon that would otherwise remain stored in the seafloor sediment for ages. Protecting 35 percent of the ocean would eliminate 28 percent of those carbon emissions and thus help reduce man-made climate change. In short, turning 35 percent— just over a third—of Earth's oceans into fully protected areas would provide immense economic benefits as well as protect vast areas of the natural world that we all love.

Our recommendations would have been counterintuitive to many in the past, but now we know that protecting more of the natural world is not only essential to our survival, but it is also a sine qua non for a prosperous economy. And we have the data, calculations, and rational argument to prove it. The long-term benefits of restoring our degraded ecosystems and protecting the wild left on our planet far exceed the short-term benefits under a status quo that continues to destroy our natural world.

CHAPTER FOURTEEN

WHY WE NEED THE WILD

O N APRIL 15, 2019, the Nôtre-Dame Cathedral in Paris burned. I was shocked as I watched on television how the flames mercilessly devoured thick oak beams, causing the collapse of the roof. Brave firefighters prevented the destruction of the whole structure. French citizens and tourists alike cried without solace on the streets of Paris. The morning after, the tragedy was on page one of newspapers all around the world. Within 48 hours, French billionaires had pledged hundreds of millions of euros for the cathedral's reconstruction, and President Emmanuel Macron committed to rebuild it within five years.

The wooden beams that supported the roof came from oaks in the Middle Ages, so large that the like could not be found in France anymore. Over the centuries, people have logged the ancient forests where those old trees grew, all throughout Europe, until now they remain standing in only a few places, like the Carpathian Mountains in Romania, or the Bialowieza Forest straddling Poland and Belarus.

I have been to both places. In the Retezat Mountains in Romania, I walked through pine forests and meadows so wild and untouched that they are among the only places left in Europe that are home to bears, wolves, and lynxes living together. I felt like I was walking in the magical Rivendell Forest, expecting an elf to appear at any moment. In Bialowieza, I marveled among oak trees a hundred feet tall, old enough to have shaded some of the last remaining wild European bison— those depicted in European cave paintings from 30,000 years ago. These last wild places are few, far apart, and disappearing. Romanian illegal loggers are clear-cutting the largest patch of intact forest in Europe, and some Polish officials are violating European Union rules and trying to log Bialowieza. But no billionaires appeared after these incidents were in the news, promising hundreds of millions of dollars to save the last old forests in Europe (notwithstanding the heroic efforts of a handful of philanthropists and conservationists). Governments are not acting effectively to stop these natural massacres, either. Why not?

Why is the world not feeling the same tragic sense of loss about our natural cathedrals? We were all touched by Nôtre-Dame—myself included—because nobody expects our historic symbols to vanish. Nôtre-Dame, the Eiffel Tower, Big Ben, the ruins of the Parthenon, to name a few: They are part of our immutable cultural landscape. We all expect them to be there. But only when these icons are at risk do most people realize that they are more than just stones and wood. These places are part of our identity as a civilization. They are global tourist destinations and, for many, sites of sacred devotion. Shouldn't the natural world be all of that, too: part of our identity, revered destinations, sacred sites?

The truth is, we need forests more than we need cathedrals. Without the natural world, there is no good food to eat, no safe water to drink, no oxygen to breathe, not even rain in many places. Everything humanity worries about, everything we count on, is built upon a healthy natural world. A degraded environment is a hotbed of all the problems affecting humanity. My friend Lee White, minister of environment of Gabon, told me that the Congo Basin forest in West Africa produces the rain that waters the highlands of Ethiopia, on the other side of the continent. If the Congo forest were destroyed, no more water—or food—in Ethiopia. That's 125 million people as of 2019, probably double that by 2050. In addition, those highlands provide the water for half of the Nile. Enter Sudan and Egypt, with an additional 138 million people, and growing. We have already seen the consequences of a region without water and food: riots, instability, collapse of governments, and massive migration to wealthier countries.

Stability and prosperity in northeastern Africa starts with a wild forest in Gabon and Congo, thanks to the work of large trees that "call the rain" and absorb massive amounts of our carbon pollution, of forest elephants and lowland gorillas that eat their large fruit and defecate their seeds a distance away, of insects and worms and fungi that degrade the recent necrosphere and turn it into nutrients that will be driven up the trees using sunlight and the water that they themselves helped to produce. A miraculous web of interactions so complex that we could never re-create it. Millions of species of microbes, fungi, plants, and animals carrying out their individual interactions—competition, predation, facilitation, symbiosis—in self-assembling systems over time (advancing along paths of ecological succession) and space (creating the mosaic of ecological communities at different stages of maturity that form the ecosystems that make up this amazing world).

The wild is here in all its baroque glory because it's what has worked throughout the history of life on our planet. Every interaction that didn't really work isn't here anymore. Only what fits in the giant puzzle remains. The irony is that the fate of all the species on which our very existence depends is in our hands. And we are squeezing them off the planet at a rate second only to the asteroid that killed the dinosaurs. We have become the asteroid. But we still can save ourselves and our natural world.

Yet some will say: "Won't we have to feed nine billion people by 2050? We have to use all that land that is now unproductive forest or grassland!" Here again is the perceived conflict between production and protection. Short-term wants and needs make food production prevail over conservation of natural ecosystems. Agriculture, forestry, and other land uses are the main driver of biodiversity loss on land and the human activity that uses up more freshwater, pollutes the rivers and ocean, and emits 24 percent of the greenhouse gases globally. If we continue on this trajectory, letting our economy eat away the intact ecosystems that keep us alive, the prospects for sustainability of our planet are grim.

If we get a little smarter about the way we eat and about the way we cultivate the land and sea, however, we can actually have both a healthy Earth and a healthy food supply without increasing the footprint of either agriculture or fisheries. How would that happen?

First, it turns out that we already produce food for 10 billion people. We just waste a third of it, from the field to the table. The economic value of global lost food amounts to one trillion dollars every year. The Food and Agriculture Organization estimates that this lost food could feed two billion people each year. On top of that, if food loss and waste were a country, it would rank as the third largest emitter of greenhouse gases. Only China and the United States would beat it.

We could eliminate much of this waste, especially in North America, Europe, and industrialized Asia, where waste predominates at the end of the supply chain. How? By not overpurchasing, by reducing oversize portions (much of which are left and wasted), and by ordering fewer takeout meals. (The third practice would also eliminate food container waste; in 2019, takeout lunches resulted in six million food containers discarded each day in China.) Less waste and slimmer waistlines seem like a good combination. We could learn to appreciate fruits and vegetables for their flavor rather than their appearance, rather than preferring the perfectly shaped, tasteless items we see in most supermarkets in the global North. A different effort would be needed in less developed countries, where food losses tend to occur closer to the farm, often before the produce even gets to the consumer. Investment in storage and refrigeration and efficient distribution systems and markets would contribute to the solution.

Second, with simple changes to our diet we could reduce our footprint—and greenhouse gas emissions—radically. Currently, a third of the global agricultural crops are used for animal feed. This is food that does not even reach humans but goes to feed our domesticated livestock. Industrialized beef is the least efficient food to raise. Typically it requires 30 kilograms (66 lb) of grain to produce a single kilogram (2.2 lb) of edible boneless beef. In addition, cows are the largest producer of methane gas, which is 25 times more potent as a greenhouse gas than carbon dioxide. In the United States, livestock production—mostly cows—takes an astonishing 41 percent of the land, mostly for grazing. A 2018 study showed that animal farming takes up 80 percent of the world's agricultural land, but it delivers only 18 percent of our calories. That means that many former grasslands and prairies have been converted to overgrazed ranges where the ecosystem stores less carbon, produces a lot of methane via cow burping and flatulence, and has lost the capacity to provide all other ecosystem benefits to us.

A "flexitarian" diet based mostly on plants, with occasional meat consumption, would deliver all nutrients our bodies need, including protein, and actually make people healthier. Small shifts from beef to poultry would also have significant benefits. And, very important, a dietary shift like this would reduce the environmental impacts of food production. The current agricultural footprint could produce 50 percent more calories and reduce greenhouse gas emissions at the same time. Land that we no longer use to produce food could then be restored as natural grasslands. We would slow or stop deforestation and reduce our agricultural demand for freshwater.

Third, we can find many ways to produce food more efficiently. Large-scale monoculture agriculture is especially egregious. Heavily subsidized by governments, industrial agriculture poisons the soil with pesticides, fungicides, insecticides, and excess fertilizer. The healthy soil with its marvelous micro-ecosystem ends up dead. Industrial agriculture overuses freshwater by irrigating arid areas and depleting aquifers much faster than nature can replenish them. Frequent tilling fractures the soil and destroys its natural structure, reducing its ability to retain water and causing the loss of fertile soil. Each year, 24 billion metric tons of soil are lost to surface runoff worldwide. To put it in perspective, every year we're losing 3.4 metric tons of soil—two cubic meters (2.6 cu yd)—for every person on our planet. And the fertilizers and other agricultural chemicals that have been pumped into that soil ultimately end up in the ocean, creating dead zones that choke out most life in them. We already have 500 of those, growing in size and number all the time.

To reverse these ominous trends, we could shift to what is called regenerative agriculture, a conservation and restoration approach to food production. Soil can be regenerated through, among other practices, reduced tilling, planting cover crops, rotating crops, and using farm waste—compost—instead of synthetic fertilizers. These age-old practices were lost when humanity shifted to industrial and chemical agricultural practices. Returning to them will succeed in regenerating topsoil and increasing biodiversity, thus enhancing productivity, providing natural pest control, and reducing water waste. The key factor is improving the health of the soil, bringing it back to that complex underground ecosystem that not only increases fertility but also retains more water, recharges aquifers, reduces soil erosion—and captures large amounts of carbon. Studies suggest that a global shift to regenerative agriculture would help to sequester much of the carbon pollution that we expel into the atmosphere, thus helping to mitigate climate change.

Fourth, in the ocean, we must address the loss of biodiversity caused by the overextraction of its living biomass. Our recent research suggests that we can protect much more of the ocean (at least 30 percent) while boosting fisheries productivity, thanks to the spillover effect of fully protected areas. In addition, we can manage fisheries sustainably in the unprotected part of the ocean through several actions. There are too many fishing vessels chasing too few fish. A World Bank report suggested that cutting fishing effort by 40 percent would increase the efficiency and profitability of fishing. We need to move from the open access regime that results in overfishing in much of the ocean to rights-based fisheries, giving fishermen a vested interest in preventing overfishing and increasing compliance with catch limits. Subsidies that perpetuate overcapacity and overfishing need to be eliminated. That would also save the world more than $35 billion annually, which could be used to restore artisanal fisheries within countries' waters. We need better aquaculture. Currently, aquaculture has enormous negative impacts by polluting the coastal environment, spreading disease, and depleting local fish populations through introduced farmed species. Therefore, aquaculture needs to abandon its current dependence on fish feed, enhance the production of seaweed and filter feeders (for example, mussels and oysters), and close its production cycle in order to avoid pollution of the marine environment. A recent study suggests that the current total catch from wild fisheries could be replaced totally by aquaculture, using less than .015 percent of the global ocean area.

Finally, global heating (euphemistically called "climate change") is an overarching threat to biodiversity, from species to ecosystems. Much has been written elsewhere on how the impacts of increased temperatures will affect life on land and at sea. A great resource is the 2019 book *Biodiversity and Climate Change: Transforming the Biosphere,* edited by my friend Tom Lovejoy.

Just to give one example, many species will not be able to tolerate future higher temperatures and will thus move toward higher altitudes and latitudes to escape the heat. This is not a theory. It is already happening. Birds, mammals, and even trees are moving higher on mountains as temperatures increase, and fish are moving from tropical to colder seas. But the species living on top of the mountains or in the Arctic will have nowhere to go as their habitats heat up, and many will go extinct. With species moving around, the ecosystems they form will change. We're already witnessing a global transformation of our biosphere at a pace much faster than it took for current ecosystems to self-assemble and evolve. This is diminishing the ability of complex ecosystems to deliver all the services we enjoy and to be resilient amid the current continuous climate disruption.

Future changes in the structure of ecosystems are likely to be abrupt, as species in a given ecosystem respond to temperatures above their tolerance limits almost simultaneously. A 2020 study suggests that if we continue on the current trajectory toward 4 °C of warming relative to pre-industrial levels, these abrupt shifts will begin before 2030 in tropical seas and by 2050 in tropical forests and higher latitudes. Protected and unprotected areas would be affected equally—temperatures do not observe such boundaries. Therefore, phasing off fossil fuels and shifting to a carbon-neutral society is a sine qua non for preserving the stability and resilience of our life-support systems.

YES, SOME WILL SAY it's all too expensive; that we cannot afford to make these changes. That's like saying we cannot afford to save ourselves. It is absurd to even ask whether we should do it or not—unless you are one of those trying to make as much money as possible in the casino of the *Titanic*—*after* hitting the iceberg.

The question was supposed to be settled once and for all with the Stern review, conducted for the Treasury of the United Kingdom in 2006 by Lord Nicholas Stern, a former chief economist of the World Bank. Stern compared the cost of responding to global heating with the cost of leaving it unchecked. He found that by responding to global heating, we would be shaving 1 to 2 percent from the world's GDP growth rate per year, whereas doing nothing would cost at least 5 percent of GDP per year. His analysis has been widely backed up since. Many countries spend 2 percent of their GDP in defense. If that's too much to spend in combating global heating, then maybe it's our current economic system that's not affordable.

Those who argue that we cannot protect more of nature say we need a balance between the needs of humankind and the needs of nature. The situation is indeed unbalanced—but in favor of humans, and especially those who overexploit nature for economic advantage. The economic growth favored by the powers that be is based on the destruction of biodiversity and the excessive use of fossil fuels, and we have been told that theirs is a better metric than measuring the actual prosperity and happiness of people. We are running our planet like a Ponzi scheme, wrote my friend Daniel Pauly of the University of British Columbia. We use capital from one investor to pay another, pretending we are sharing a profit, and then need to find a new investor to pay the former. But a Ponzi scheme works only as long as there are new investors to fool. Once the pyramid becomes too large and we run out of new investors, the whole construct collapses. Ditto for our land and ocean. We're running out of forests to destroy and fishing grounds to empty. But we do not need to tap the last ones to realize that this growth-based construct is unsustainable. Consumption grows, but our planet and the number of other creatures within do not. Now is the time to repair the damage we have done to our brothers and sisters throughout nature, and give them more space, so they can heal—and heal us along the way.

So what do we need to do to conserve the wild that we so desperately need in our lives? Studies suggest that half of the planet should be protected—both for the preservation of most creatures on Earth and also for us to obtain maximum benefits from the natural world. We are far from that goal.

To date, only 15 percent of the land on Earth is protected, and only 7 percent of the ocean has been designated or proposed for protection. We have a long way to go, but it is possible. Some countries have already protected large fractions of their land (for example, Bhutan has protected 60 percent; Venezuela, 54 percent). Others have already protected large fractions of the seas they control (for example, Palau has protected 80 percent; Chile, 42 percent; Niue, 40 percent; the

United Kingdom, 30 percent; the Seychelles, 30 percent; Gabon, 28 percent). These countries are leading the way in making more space for nature to survive and thrive.

In 2021, the countries of the world will meet under the auspices of the United Nations Convention on Biological Diversity (CBD) to decide how much space we are all willing to give to the natural world. At the National Geographic Society, alongside our colleagues at the Wyss Campaign for Nature, we have been pushing for a global target of at least 30 percent of the planet—land and sea—protected by 2030, proposing that as a milestone on the way to protecting half of Earth so it can return to its natural state of health and productivity. We believe that 30 percent protected by 2030 is the minimum, and unnegotiable. As I write these lines, leading countries are building a High Ambition Coalition for Nature and People, chaired by the governments of Costa Rica and France, that is pushing for 30 percent by 2030 as an apex target for the CBD framework. Recent surveys around the world show that citizens believe that we have already protected 30 percent of Earth, and overwhelmingly express their desire to see half of the planet protected. The science and the economics are clear, leading governments are responding to the urgency, and people are asking for it.

IN 1949, Aldo Leopold wrote of a land ethic that "enlarges the boundaries of the community to include soils, waters, plants, and animals, or collectively: the land." Now we know that the community encompasses the entire biosphere: the land, the seas, and even the atmosphere. We have learned enough about the nature of nature to know that every living being on our planet, including ourselves, is linked in complex and inextricable ways to other living beings, no matter where their home is. Therefore, it is time for us to move beyond a land ethic to a planetary ethic. Let us all envision the overview effect experienced by astronauts who have seen Earth from space, understanding that it makes no sense to base our behavior on a set of ethics that applies only to our most immediate social network, and that we must see ourselves as part of an integrated whole, interconnected to, dependent on, and responsible for the entire natural world. It's our moral imperative.

This will be a transformation as revolutionary as the discovery that Earth orbits the sun, not the other way around. The planetary ethic moves humans away from a self-proclaimed center of the world and into a humble and respectful membership in the greater biosphere. It moves us from a position *over* the natural world to a place *within* it. Because of our higher intelligence, we also carry a great deal of responsibility—but that is not the same as dominion over all creatures. Now is the time to use our intelligence and compassion to protect the right of all other creatures to exist. Our reward will be the sense of awe and wonder we enjoy by living in this diverse and beautiful world.

THE NATURE OF CORONAVIRUS

S HORTLY AFTER THIS BOOK was fully edited and on its way to the printer, our world was shocked by a pandemic the likes of which no one in our generation had ever seen. COVID-19, caused by a novel coronavirus (named SARS-CoV-2), pushed the brakes on our accelerated lifestyle. Planes stopped flying, bars and restaurants closed, and people were told to stay home and not mingle. Boundaries between countries, historically drawn by military actions, lost their meaning as an invisible enemy trespassed into them all. Now drops of saliva or a cough—instead of tanks or missiles—threaten the world's major powers and their economies. The world has been brought to a standstill by a tiny virus that appears to have been transmitted to humans in late 2019 via wildlife at a "wet market" in Wuhan, China, where recently butchered meat and live wild animals are sold for food and medicine. A microscopic strand of genetic material inside a protein shield has humbled us, the hyperkeystone predator of planet Earth.

How and why did a virus jump from a wild animal to a human? What animals are the sources of these viruses? What are the ecological implications of this pandemic? What can we do to prevent the next one? Many are the questions that come to one's mind after the initial shock and denial. The last stage of grief, acceptance, must come with a deep understanding of why we got here and what we can do about it. The explanations are here, implied throughout this book, but circumstances have forced me to add this chapter, unforeseeable as I began writing. Ironically and tragically, it will make the strongest argument for why biodiversity is necessary for human health—and, ultimately, human survival.

Let's begin with the origins of the pandemic. At the time I am writing these lines, the best scientific thinking posits that the novel coronavirus originated in horseshoe bats. Bats, once again, appear to be the source of a deadly virus. Today, it is the infamous COVID-19; yesterday it was SARS (severe acute respiratory syndrome), MERS (Middle East respiratory syndrome), Ebola, and rabies—all "zoonotic" viruses, meaning they are transmitted from other animals into humans. But how did a virus spill over from bats to humans?

Viruses can mutate and mix their genetic material with that of their host and evolve quickly, which is how they tend to overwhelm their hosts' pathogen-fighting abilities. Bats are considered reservoirs for these viruses, but these little flying mammals have powerful immune systems. As they fight off viruses, they shed them in their saliva, urine, and feces. It's part of their natural way of overcoming whatever disease the virus might carry.

It seems that bat viruses need to mutate through an intermediate host—a stepping-stone of sorts—before they become a danger to us. Researchers have sequenced the genome of SARS-CoV-2 and found it closely related to other betacoronaviruses of bat origin. The differences in this virus's genetic sequence cause researchers to speculate that the intermediate host between bats and us for SARS-CoV-2 was likely Malayan pangolins—based on the best scientific evidence available at the time of this writing. Pangolins are scaly anteaters, the most illegally traded mammal in the world, coveted by folks who eat their meat or believe their scales have medicinal properties and pay up to $3,000 a kilogram for them. Now genetic research is suggesting that pangolins served as the conduit for a bat virus to invade the human world.

IN 1999, I visited the Gomantong Caves in Borneo. As I entered the massive cavern, an acrid smell punched me in the nose. It was the smell of the guano produced by more than a quarter million bats over many decades—guano that had accumulated on the ground as a soft carpet, who knows how deep. Hundreds of thousands of bats leave that cave daily on their foraging excursions, thus raining excrement over the jungle. Imagine a little pangolin going about on his daily search for ants or termites, stepping on a bat dropping or smelling it while looking for prey. That's how a pangolin could acquire bat viruses in the wild.

Or the intermediate host—be it a pangolin or any other hapless creature captured alive—could get the virus from bats at a market where both are sold. Another recent coronavirus-borne respiratory disease, the infamous SARS, also appears to have originated at a Chinese market where Asian palm civets were sold. Civets are felines, catlike mammals with short legs, a long tail, sometimes beautiful mottled patterns, and a racoonlike face mask giving them a bandit look. Palm civets appear to have contracted the SARS coronavirus from bats.

Animals such as palm civets and pangolins are captured in African or Asian tropical forests and transported alive—sometimes thousands of miles—to wet markets, where they are kept in crowded conditions, in contact with many other species. My friend, the great nature writer David Quammen, visited one of these markets in China after the SARS pandemic of 2003 and said: "I saw a ton of wild birds of all sorts that had been captured, not for pets but for food, and all caged in a great jumble, with water flowing and blood flowing, and butchery happening in a pretty unhygienic environment."

How can the virus spread from these animals to people? A person in the market can grab an animal to sell it. A person can grab an animal as he buys it. An animal can bite a person. A market cleaner might get in contact with animal blood. Anyone in the market can be sprayed with urine or blood from an animal being butchered or carried in or out of the market, and any of these people can then touch their face or shake somebody else's hand. Or the animal can become someone's dinner. The spread of the virus among humans, starting in these markets and then widening out in our crowded cities and globally connected society, is then inevitable.

People have been acquiring harmful viruses and bacteria from contact with animals in the wild for millennia. Plagues of the past caused by rats and fleas caused millions of deaths, like the Justinian plague in 541–42 that killed up to 100 million people, or the Black Death that killed up to a third of Europe's population in 1347–1352. Those rats had adapted very well— and become very abundant—in the degraded environment around the human settlements of medieval Europe.

A 2020 study explored the link between the abundance of species that carry zoonotic viruses and the likelihood of spillover to humans. They combed the scientific literature, obtained data on 142 zoonotic viruses, and found that rodents, primates, and bats carried more zoonotic viruses than other species. In fact, these groups were implicated as hosts for 76 percent of the zoonotic viruses described to date. The researchers also found that the risk of virus transmission to humans was highest from animals that had increased in abundance because they have adapted to human-dominated environments—like the rats in medieval Europe.

As humans encroach upon wild habitats, animals are more likely to interact with humans. In Uganda, for instance, a growing human population is cultivating farms closer to the forest, pushing the asymmetrical boundary between agriculture and mature ecosystems and creating more tension along it. That process includes clearing patches of forest in Kibale National Park, for example, home to chimpanzees.

Chimpanzees are highly intelligent species, our closest kin, and thus cannot resist the temptation of helping themselves to maize growing in plantations, some even inside the park. Those chimpanzees conduct night raids, yet contact with humans is inevitable. Contact occurs not only with chimpanzees but also with other primates. Around Kibale, interviews with locals revealed a boy had been bitten by a colobus monkey and a woman had moved the dead body of a vervet monkey out of a cornfield. As humans expand into the natural habitat of wild primates, we compete for water, food, and territory. Conflict—and physical contact—is unavoidable as we humans relentlessly expand into nature.

FARMS INTRUDE UPON FORESTS, and loggers and miners push into pristine ecosystems. We cut down forests for crops and livestock, drain wetlands for urban development, and flood valleys for dams. Hunters venture into once remote forests for food, or poachers kill wild animals for consumption or trap them for the illegal wildlife trade. Miners venture into tropical forests in the Congo Basin to mine coltan, a rare mineral that is a key component of the cell phone you and I carry in our pocket. As we humans venture more deeply into what was once wild, we not only disrupt ecosystems but also stress the animals inhabiting them. As more of us come into contact with stressed or infected animals, we increase our chances of being exposed to new diseases for which we have no immunity.

Today we are also building perfect hotbeds of infectious diseases, even in temperate countries where bush meat—meat from terrestrial wild animals—is very seldom eaten and animal products are not sold as medicine. Close to my home, the forests in the eastern United States have been coming back after massive deforestation by English settlers starting in the late 1500s. But what has not yet come back is the native keystone predator—the gray wolf—which was hunted to ecological extinction in the region centuries ago. The removal of the top predator started a trophic cascade with ultimate consequences to human health today.

After wolves were decimated in the eastern United States, coyote populations increased. That in turn increased coyote predation on red foxes, which showed a regional decline. Red foxes are a major predator of small rodents, which are intermediate hosts of the nymphs of ticks that transmit Lyme disease to humans. Fewer wolves, more coyotes; more coyotes, fewer foxes; fewer foxes, more rodents; more rodents, more ticks. The increased availability of hosts for tick nymphs means that more ticks will become adults and jump onto deer, which are also more abundant because of the absence of their main predator—the gray wolf. A link has been suggested between a boom in deer populations and Lyme disease, but research suggests that the incidence of Lyme disease more likely jumped due to the increased abundance of small mammals caused by that wolf–coyote–fox–small rodent trophic cascade. One empirical proof of this hypothesis is that Lyme disease is rare in western New York, where foxes are abundant, even though the region has a large deer population.

What about the mammals we eat—cows, pigs, and goats—which account for 60 percent of the biomass of all land mammals? Can we get diseases from them? The answer is yes. As a matter of fact, livestock carry eight times more zoonotic diseases than wild mammals. The high abundance of domesticated mammals and the crowded environments in which they are raised make our main source of animal food a risk to our health. In 2009, for example, a novel influenza virus (H1N1) spilled over from pigs to humans in Mexico, causing a local outbreak and then spreading rapidly to become a global pandemic. Researchers found that the virus was a mix of a swine virus from North America (which had jumped from birds to pigs) and another swine virus from Europe. It appears that the new virus stayed locally in Mexico for 10 years before it developed the ability to spill over to humans.

AND WHAT ABOUT THE CREATURES in the ocean— the other 70 percent of the planet? Does our exploitation of ocean life also threaten human health? I discovered the answer during our exploration of some of the most remote islands in the central Pacific.

The Nature of Coronavirus

In 2005, I organized my first research expedition to Kingman Reef and neighboring islands. Kingman is the northernmost of the Line Islands, 11 coral islands that stretch 2,350 kilometers (1,460 miles) across the Equator, 930 nautical miles south of Honolulu. During that first expedition—which planted the seed in my mind for Pristine Seas, developed years later—we visited four of these islands north of the Equator. They provided the perfect natural experiment to compare different levels of human impact on coral reefs.

Kingman was uninhabited. The next island to the south, Palmyra, had 20 people manning a research station and taking care of the Palmyra Atoll National Wildlife Refuge. Farther south were Teraina (with 900 people at the time), Tabuaeran (2,500 people), and Kiritimati (5,000 people), which are part of the Republic of Kiribati. These four islands were close enough together to share oceanographic and climate conditions, flora, and fauna. The variable that changed across the islands—the experimental treatment—was the number of humans present.

Excited about the opportunity, I put together a team of scientists to assess the diversity and abundance of everything from small to large—viruses, bacteria, algae, invertebrates, and fish—and to measure how the coral reef ecosystem changes along a gradient of human disturbance. In five weeks, we conducted 620 person-dives and counted and estimated the abundance and biomass of everything we could. What we found was clear: As soon as you have people fishing, even just several hundred, they trim the food web from the top. And as the number of people increases from none to just a few thousand, the coral reef shifts from one with lots of sharks and corals to one without sharks but with lots of small fish and seaweed.

We made another discovery I had not expected about the smallest creatures on the reef, though.

I will never regret inviting my dear friend Forest Rohwer to join the expedition. Forest is a brilliant microbiologist at San Diego State University and among the first to use genomic technology to study viruses and bacteria in the ocean. That year in the Line Islands, Forest and his small team collected water samples to measure microbe abundances along the human gradient. They found 10 times more bacteria in the water in Kiritimati than in Kingman.

Not only the microbial numbers increased with increasing numbers of people, but also what bacteria did changed dramatically. At Kingman, we found crystal clear waters, where half the microbes were very small bacteria like *Prochlorococcus,* which simply photosynthesize for a living, whereas at Kiritimati, we found murky waters, where about a third of the bacteria were pathogens, including several types of *Staphylococcus, Vibrio,* and *Escherichia.* Especially worrying was *Vibrio,* which can cause diseases in corals, contributing to the shift from coral-dominated to seaweed-dominated reefs, which in turn enhances microbial blooms. *Vibrio* can also cause fatal diseases in humans such as cholera, gastroenteritis, wound infections, and septicemia. Forest calls this ecosystem shift—from mature, stable, and full of large animals to immature and dominated by small creatures—the "microbialization" of coral reefs.

In April and May 2009, I returned to the Line Islands as we conducted the first National Geographic Pristine Seas expedition to five islands south of the Equator, all uninhabited. There we found what we had found at Kingman: clean water and extremely high fish biomass, including many sharks, and a reef dominated by living coral. When we made our way into the lagoon of Millennium Atoll, we marveled at the abundance of giant clams, with iridescent blues and greens—something we had also observed in the lagoon at Kingman.

Giant clams filter water through their bodies and capture microorganisms from it for food. They are natural water filters, and we wondered how much they helped to keep the water that clean. Forest collected water from the lagoon and filled experimental aquaria on board our ship: some with a living giant clam in them, some with an empty clamshell, and some with nothing but water. Then he measured the abundance of bacteria over time.

The results were astonishing. The giant clams removed most bacteria from the seawater within 12 hours, while the water in the other aquaria became turbid and loaded with microbes. Forest then added *Vibrio* to each aquarium, from a culture he had brought with him on the expedition. (Who else travels with *Vibrio?*) As expected, the giant clams significantly reduced the abundance of *Vibrio* in the experimental aquaria, compared with the control aquaria, where

Vibrio thrived. Another example of how nature provides antidotes that we are only now recognizing: Giant clams have been harvested for meat and shells from most reefs in the Pacific, to the point that they are practically gone in many places. People have unknowingly been removing natural filters—the N95 masks of the lagoon—that were protecting them against disease.

WE ARE ALL IN THIS TOGETHER, all species on the planet, as we learned when Nadia, a tiger at New York's Bronx Zoo, tested positive for SARS-CoV-2. She seems to have been infected by a zookeeper carrying the virus but showing no symptoms. Our closest relatives, chimpanzees and gorillas, are also at risk. We don't know if they can be affected by SARS-CoV-2, but they are known to be susceptible to other human respiratory diseases. To prevent spillover from humans to mountain gorillas, Virunga National Park in the Democratic Republic of the Congo and Volcanoes National Park in Rwanda closed their doors to tourists in late March 2020. Mountain gorillas live in family groups that seldom meet others, but infection of a single animal could wipe out a whole family group in a matter of weeks. There are slightly more than a thousand mountain gorillas left on the planet, so every family group matters.

So, what can we do? While the world ought to double down to help those in need now, we might also start thinking about how to prevent the next zoonotic pandemic. As soon as COVID-19 was traced back to bats, some on social media were quick to propose that the solution is to exterminate them. But proposals to exterminate bats—or civets, or pangolins, or any other wild animal that has been the source or carrier of recent novel infectious diseases—simply prove our ignorance of how the natural world works.

In this book we have seen, again and again, that even though we don't know what most of them do, all wild animals have important jobs that keep our biosphere running. Bats contribute to ecosystems in ways that yield many benefits for people. They are voracious insect-eaters with the potential to keep malaria-carrying mosquito populations under control and to reduce agricultural pests, thus helping farmers. The mammalian equivalent of bees, bats pollinate more than 258 species of plants, including important crops such as bananas, mangos, breadfruits, agave, and durians. Researchers have estimated the global economic value of bats' pollination service at $200 billion. And still we have more to learn from these amazing animals: mammals that fly at night, navigating with biological radar. Some hunt insects, others eat fruit or suck nectar from flowers, and others fish in rivers. How extraordinary!

If we have learned anything from our study of natural ecosystems as it applies to these recent diseases, it is that instead of exterminating wild animals to stop the passage of disease to people, we should do the opposite: We should safeguard the natural ecosystems that are their homes and, if needed, help to set them back on their path to maturity through rewilding. Again and again, researchers have found that when we degrade habitats, animals such as bats, pangolins, civets, and chimpanzees become stressed and shed more viruses. On the other hand, forests with a diversity of microbial, plant, and animal species harbor less disease. Biodiversity dilutes any viruses that emerge, whether from bat feces or any other sources. Same thing we found on coral reefs. Biodiversity provides a natural shield that absorbs the fallout from pathogens, and all this happens without our interference. A healthy natural world is our best antivirus.

At the same time, we need to improve economic conditions for people so that they don't have to cut and burn forests in desperation for subsistence farming, which only exacerbates the problem. We need to ban trade in wildlife, whether for meat, medicine, or captive pets. Of course, the usual suspects will argue that we cannot afford to protect more of the natural world or ban wildlife trade. But let's look at the numbers. A recent economic report led by Anthony Waldron at the University of Cambridge estimated that a system of protected areas covering 30 percent of the planet could cost between $103 billion and $171 billion a year, depending on location. That is just a fraction of the trillions of dollars of losses the COVID-19 pandemic is inflicting on the world economy—in addition to all the human losses. Prevention—investing in nature—is a much safer, cheaper, and smarter investment than having to respond to the next pandemic.

The Nature of Coronavirus

This pandemic is the loudest reminder for humanity that we are all connected in our biosphere, that our actions on one part of the planet can affect every other part of it. Think about it: It may have taken only one person at a wet market to create a pandemic. Many may think individual actions don't matter, but COVID-19 has proved them wrong.

In ancient times, smaller human groups and restricted mobility probably kept diseases local. But over the course of history, humanity has made it very easy for viruses to become evolutionarily successful. We gather in great densities in our built ecosystems and move around the globe like no other species ever has before. We have built asymmetrical boundaries, but we have also removed many others. We have turned wild habitats into cities, farmland, and shopping malls, crowding in on the species with whom we share this planet. We have created the perfect conditions for a modern plague.

COVID-19 is yet another reminder that conservation is not just a luxury for rich countries or a romantic ideal. Our very survival depends on our being better members of the biosphere, our larger community. Viruses are part of the biosphere, too—more diverse and abundant than all the bacteria, plants, and animals combined. At least 230,000 different types of viruses infect mammals alone. Some can be deadly to humans, but others are beneficial. For example, bacteriophages—viruses that infect and destroy specific bacteria—can be found in the mucous membrane linings of our digestive, respiratory, and reproductive tracts and form part of our natural immune system, providing a barrier against bacteria that could infect our bodies. Current medical research is investigating the use of bacteriophages to destroy antibiotic-resistant bacteria that could be fatal to humans. Cancer researchers are also exploring alternative therapies using viruses to kill cancer cells selectively, an alternative to radiation or chemotherapy. Like other microbes intrinsic to our bodies, viruses blur the line between us and the rest of the biosphere.

Still, harmful viruses, bacteria, and other pathogens are not going away. We can reduce the spread of diseases and promote the abundance of healthful microbes in many ways, but killing bats—or any other wild animals that are viral hosts—is not one of them. Clamping down on the trade and consumption of wildlife, ending deforestation, protecting intact ecosystems, educating people about the risks of consuming wildlife, changing the way we produce food, phasing off fossil fuels, and transitioning to a circular economy: These are the things we can and must do.

We need to build for stability and resilience instead of unfettered growth. The protection of our natural world is the inoculation we need, right now, before it's too late. Even if it's just for selfish reasons—for our own survival—now more than ever, we need the wild.

ACKNOWLEDGMENTS

A BOOK IS LIKE AN ECOSYSTEM: It is the product of many interactions, some known to us, some unknown. Yet, as in an ecosystem, they all work to make things happen.

The idea for this book came after 30 years of thinking about ecological succession—first in a classroom at the University of Barcelona, and later while seeing humans reverse succession and protected areas restart it. The giants I had the fortune of interacting with, during my academic years and after, taught me the ecological principles described in this book and directed me to wonderful classic sources. Special shout-outs go to Kike Ballesteros, Charles-François Boudouresque, Paul Dayton, Jim Estes, Mike Fay, Alan Friedlander, Josep M. Gili, Jo Harmelin, Mireille Harmelin- Vivien, Jeremy Jackson, Nancy Knowlton, Tom Lovejoy, Jane Lubchenco, Enrique Macpherson, Ramón Margalef, Bob Paine, Daniel Pauly, Lluís Polo, Forest Rohwer, Ed Wilson, Boris Worm, and Mikel Zabala. They are poets of nature, who helped me deepen my love for the natural world beyond facts and statistics. To all of them—and many others—I will always be grateful. Isabella Tree is an inspiration who provided precious comments to the manuscript.

I am indebted to the National Geographic Society for more than a decade of trust and support. To the National Geographic Pristine Seas team, and to the National Geographic–Wyss Campaign for Nature team, thank you for working so tirelessly to help save the wild nature we need so desperately. You are a continuous inspiration to me, as are my friends and colleagues who dedicate their lives to save and restore the wild across the world.

This book was written to help continue our conservation work that has been supported so generously by many partners and friends, especially the Prince Albert II of Monaco Foundation; Bjork; Blancpain; Miguel Bosé; The Keith Campbell Foundation for the Environment; Jean and Steve Case; John Codey; the Leonardo DiCaprio Foundation; Roger and Rosemary Enrico; Google; Loic Gouzer; the Helmsley Charitable Trust; Sven Lindblad; Ann Luskey; the Oracle Education Foundation; Jean and Tom Rutherfoord; Vicki, Roger, and Shari Sant; the Philip Stephenson Foundation; the van Rappard family; Leonor Varela; the Waitt Foundation; the Wyss Foundation; and many individual donors. I cannot thank you enough for your commitment to save the wild.

Deep thanks to Pope Francis, Cardinal Peter Turkson, and Fr. Augusto Zampini for awakening in me the importance of spirituality for saving the natural world.

This book would not have been published without the enthusiastic support, encouragement, and advice from Lisa Thomas—the wonderful head of National Geographic Books—and Susan Hitchcock—my wonderful editor, who greatly improved my writing. Writing a book with you is more fun than one could think. Thank you for being such great partners. Thanks also to Jane Sunderland for her thorough copyediting. I am grateful to my friend Jennifer Jacquet for her advice on how to conceive, pitch, and write a book.

Finally, I cannot thank enough my life co-pilot, Kristin Rechberger—my keystone—who is my greatest mentor and makes my life as diverse and wonderful as the wildest jungle or coral reef.

KEY
REFERENCES

Information about National Geographic Pristine Seas is available online at pristineseas.org.

CHAPTER 1: RE-CREATING NATURE

Bar-On, Y. M., R. Phillips, and R. Milo. "The Biomass Distribution on Earth." *Proceedings of the National Academy of Sciences* 115, no. 25 (2018): 6506–11.

Burgess, T. B., V. D. Marino, and J. Joyce. Internal report of the Biosphere 2 Science and Research Department. Biodiversity Working Group Summary, August 11–12, 1996.

Dempsey, R. C., ed. *The International Space Station: Operating an Outpost in the New Frontier.* Government Printing Office, 2017.

Díaz, S., J. Settele, E. Brondizio, eds. *Summary for Policymakers of the Global Assessment Report on Biodiversity and Ecosystem Services of the Intergovernmental Science-Policy Platform on Biodiversity and Ecosystem Services.* IPBES Secretariat, 2019.

Grooten, M., and R. E. A. Almond, eds. *Living Planet Report—2018: Aiming Higher.* World Wildlife Fund, 2018.

Intergovernmental Panel on Climate Change (IPCC). *Climate Change and Land: An IPCC Special Report on Climate Change, Desertification, Land Degradation, Sustainable Land Management, Food Security, and Greenhouse Gas Fluxes in Terrestrial Ecosystems.* IPCC, 2019. Available online at www.ipcc.ch/srccl-report-download-page/.

Montanarella, L., R. Scholes, and A. Brainich, eds. *The IPBES Assessment Report on Land Degradation and Restoration.* IPBES Secretariat, 2018.

Walter, A., and S. C. Lambrecht. "Biosphere 2 Center as a Unique Tool for Environmental Studies." *Journal of Environmental Monitoring* 6, no. 4 (2004): 267–77.

CHAPTER 2: WHAT'S AN ECOSYSTEM?

Pickett, S. T., and J. M. Grove. "Urban Ecosystems: What Would Tansley Do?" *Urban Ecosystems* 12, no. 1 (2009): 1–8.

Sanderson, E. W. *Mannahatta: A Natural History of New York City.* Abrams, 2013.

Tansley, A. G. "The Use and Abuse of Vegetational Concepts and Terms." *Ecology* 16, no. 3 (1935): 284–307.

Weisman, A. *The World Without Us.* Macmillan, 2008.

CHAPTER 3: THE SMALLEST ECOSYSTEM

D'Ancona, U. *Dell'influenza della stasi peschereccia del periodo 1914–18 sul patrimonio ittico dell'Alto Adriatico.* Comitato Talassografico Italiano, 1926.

Darwin, C. *On the Origin of Species by Means of Natural Selection, or the Preservation of*

Favoured Races in the Struggle for Life. John Murray, 1859.

Gause, G. F. *The Struggle for Existence.* Williams and Wilkins, 1934.

Volterra, V. "Variations and Fluctuations of the Number of Individuals in Animal Species Living Together." *ICES Journal of Marine Science* 3, no. 1 (1928): 3–51.

CHAPTER 4: SUCCESSION

Clements, F. E. *Plant Succession: An Analysis of the Development of Vegetation.* Carnegie Institution of Washington, 1916.

Connell, J. H., and R. O. Slatyer. "Mechanisms of Succession in Natural Communities and Their Role in Community Stability and Organization. *The American Naturalist* 111, no. 982 (1977): 1119–44.

Grigg, R. W., and J. E. Maragos. "Recolonization of Hermatypic Corals on Submerged Lava Flows in Hawaii." *Ecology* 55, no. 2 (1974): 387–95.

Margalef, R., 1963. "On Certain Unifying Principles in Ecology." *American Naturalist* 97, no. 897 (1963): 357–74.

———. *Our Biosphere.* Vol. 10 of *Excellence in Ecology.* Ecology Institute, 1997.

Odum, E. "The Strategy of Ecosystem Development." *Science* 164, no. 3877 (1969): 262–70.

Pandolfi, J. M., and J. B. Jackson. "Ecological Persistence Interrupted in Caribbean Coral Reefs." *Ecology Letters* 9, no. 7 (2006): 818–26.

Putts, M. R., F. A. Parrish, F. A. Trusdell, and S. E. Kahng. "Structure and Development of Hawaiian Deep-Water Coral Communities on Mauna Loa Lava Flows." *Marine Ecology Progress Series* 630 (2019): 69–82.

CHAPTER 5: BOUNDARIES

Berthold, P. *Bird Migration: A General Survey.* Oxford University Press, 2001.

Davis, W. "The World Until Yesterday by Jared Diamond—Review." The *Guardian* (Jan. 9, 2013).

Margalef, R. *Ecologia.* Ediciones Omega, 1974.

———. *Our Biosphere.* Vol. 10 of *Excellence in Ecology.* Ecology Institute, 1997.

Stiglitz, J. E., A. Sen, and J. P. Fitoussi. *Mismeasuring Our Lives: Why GDP Doesn't Add Up.* The New Press, 2010.

Van Der Lingen, C. D., J. C. Coetzee, and L. Hutchings. "Overview of the KwaZulu-Natal Sardine Run." *African Journal of Marine Science* 32, no. 2 (2010): 271–77.

CHAPTER 6: ARE ALL SPECIES EQUAL?

Ballesteros, E. *Els vegetals i la zonació litoral: espècies, comunitats i factors que influeixen en la seva distribució.* Vol. 101. Institut d'Estudis Catalans, 1992.

Dayton, P. K. "Toward an Understanding of Community Resilience and the Potential Effects of Enrichments to the Benthos at McMurdo Sound, Antarctica." In *Proceedings of the Colloquium on Conservation Problems in Antarctica,* edited by B. C. Parker, 81–96. Allen Press, 1972.

———. 1985. "Ecology of Kelp Communities." *Annual Review of Ecology and Systematics* 16, no. 1 (1985): 215–45.

Estes, J. *Serendipity: An Ecologist's Quest to Understand Nature.* University of California Press, 2016.

Estes, J. A., N. S. Smith, and J. F. Palmisano. "Sea Otter Predation and Community Organization in the Western Aleutian Islands, Alaska." *Ecology* 59, no. 4 (1978): 822–33.

Estes, J. A., J. Terborgh, J. S. Brashares, M. E. Power, J. Berger, W. J. Bond, S. R. Carpenter, et al. "Trophic Downgrading of Planet Earth." *Science* 333, no. 6040 (2011): 301–306.

Estes, J. A., M. T. Tinker, T. M. Williams, and D. F. Doak. "Killer Whale Predation on Sea Otters Linking Oceanic and Nearshore Ecosystems." *Science* 282, no. 5388 (1998): 473–76.

Howard Hughes Medical Institute (HHMI). "Some Animals Are More Equal Than Others: Keystone Species and Trophic Cascades." Biointeractive video. HHMI, 2016. Available online at naturedocu

mentaries.org/14877/animals-equal-others
-keystone-species-trophic-cascades-hhmi
-2016/.

Hughes, T. P. "Catastrophes, Phase Shifts, and Large-Scale Degradation of a Caribbean Coral Reef." *Science* 265, no. 5178 (1994): 1547–51.

Paine, R. T. "Food Web Complexity and Species Diversity." *American Naturalist* 100, no. 910 (1966): 65–75.

———. "Trophic Control of Production in a Rocky Intertidal Community." *Science* 296, no. 5568 (2001): 736–39.

Sala, E., C. F. Boudouresque, and M. Harmelin-Vivien. "Fishing, Trophic Cascades, and the Structure of Algal Assemblages: Evaluation of an Old but Untested Paradigm." *Oikos* 82, no. 3 (1998): 425–39.

Sala, E., and M. Zabala. "Fish Predation and the Structure of the Sea Urchin *Paracentrotus lividus* Populations in the NW Mediterranean." *Marine Ecology Progress Series* 140, no. 1/3 (1996): 71–81.

Terborgh, J., and J. A. Estes, eds. *Trophic Cascades: Predators, Prey, and the Changing Dynamics of Nature.* Island Press, 2013.

CHAPTER 7: THE BIOSPHERE

Bristow, C. S., K. A. Hudson-Edwards, and A. Chappell. "Fertilizing the Amazon and Equatorial Atlantic With West African Dust." *Geophysical Research Letters* 37, no. 14 (2010).

Chisholm, S. W., R. J. Olson, E. R. Zettler, R. Goericke, J. B. Waterbury, and N. A. Welschmeyer. "A Novel Free-Living Prochlorophyte Abundant in the Oceanic Euphotic Zone." *Nature* 334, no. 6180 (1998): 340.

Crisp, A., C. Boschetti, M. Perry, A. Tunnacliffe, and G. Micklem. "Expression of Multiple Horizontally Acquired Genes Is a Hallmark of Both Vertebrate and Invertebrate Genomes." *Genome Biology* 16 (2015): 50.

Dewar, W. K., R. J. Bingham, R. L. Iverson, D. P. Nowacek, L. C. St. Laurent, and P. H. Wiebe. "Does the Marine Biosphere Mix the Ocean?" *Journal of Marine Research* 64 (2006): 541–61.

Garrido, D., D. C. Dallas, and D. A. Mills. "Consumption of Human Milk Glycoconjugates by Infant-Associated Bifidobacteria: Mechanisms and Implications." *Microbiology* 159 (2013; Pt. 4): 649–64.

Gorshkov, V. G., and A. M. Makar'eva. "The Biotic Atmospheric Moisture Pump: Its Relationship to Global Atmospheric Circulation and Significance for Water Turnover on Land." Preprint no. 2655 of Petersburg Nuclear Physics Institute, Gatchina, 2006.

Huang, Y. J., and H. J. Boushey. "The Microbiome and Asthma." *Annals of the American Thoracic Society* 11 (2014; Suppl. 1): S48–S51.

Kelly, J. R., Y. Borre, C. O'Brien, E. Patterson, S. El Aidy, J. Deane, P. J. Kennedy, et al. "Transferring the Blues: Depression-Associated Gut Microbiota Induces Neurobehavioural Changes in the Rat." *Journal of Psychiatric Research* 82 (2016): 109–18.

Locey, K. J., and J. T. Lennon. "Scaling Laws Predict Global Microbial Diversity." *Proceedings of the National Academy of Sciences* 113, no. 21 (2016): 5970–75.

Lovelock, J. E., and L. Margulis. "Atmospheric Homeostasis by and for the Biosphere: The Gaia Hypothesis." *Tellus* 26, no. 1/2 (1974): 2–10.

Mikkelsen, K. H., F. K. Knop, M. Frost, J. Hallas, and A. Pottegård. "Use of Antibiotics and Risk of Type 2 Diabetes: A Population-Based Case-Control Study." *Journal of Clinical Endocrinology & Metabolism* 100 (2015): 10.

Nicol, S., A. Bowie, S. Jarman, D. Lannuzel, K. M. Meiners, and P. Van Der Merwe. "Southern Ocean Iron Fertilization by Baleen Whales and Antarctic Krill." *Fish and Fisheries* 11, no. 2 (2010): 203–09.

Pennisi, E. "The Secret Life of Fungi." *Science* 304, no. 5677 (2004): 1620–22.

Qian, J., D. Hospodsky, N. Yamamoto, W. W. Nazaroff, and J. Peccia. "Size-Resolved Emission Rates of Airborne Bacteria and Fungi in an Occupied Classroom." *Indoor Air* 22, no. 4 (2012): 339–51.

Sender, R., S. Fuchs, and R. Milo. "Revised

Estimates for the Number of Human and Bacteria Cells in the Body." *PLoS Biology* 14, no. 8 (2016): e1002533.

Simard, S. W. "How Trees Talk to Each Other." Presentation at TED Summit, June 2016 Available online at www.ted.com/talks/suzanne_simard_how_trees_talk_to_each_other/.

Simard, S. W., and D. M. Durall. "Mycorrhizal Networks: A Review of Their Extent, Function, and Importance." *Canadian Journal of Botany* 82, no. 8 (2004): 1140–65.

Sugden, A., R. Stone, and C. Ash. "Ecology in the Underworld." *Science* 304, no. 5677 (2004): 1613.

Wohlleben, P. *The Hidden Life of Trees: What They Feel, How They Communicate—Discoveries From a Secret World*. Greystone Books, 2014.

CHAPTER 8: HOW ARE WE DIFFERENT?

Bolton, J. R., and D. O. Hall. "The Maximum Efficiency of Photosynthesis." *Photochemistry and Photobiology* 53, no. 4 (1991): 545–48.

Buxton, R. T., M. F. McKenna, D. Mennitt, K. Fristrup, K. Crooks, L. Angeloni, and G. Wittemyer. "Noise Pollution Is Pervasive in U.S. Protected Areas." *Science* 356, no. 6337 (2017): 531–33.

Darimont, C. T., C. H. Fox, H. M. Bryan, and T. E. Reimchen. "The Unique Ecology of Human Predators." *Science* 349, no. 6250 (2015): 858–60.

Darwin, C. *The Descent of Man, and Selection in Relation to Sex*. John Murray, 1871.

Desforges, J.-P., A. Hall, B. McConnell, A. Rosing-Asvid, J. L. Barber, A. Brownlow, S. De Guise, et al. "Predicting Global Killer Whale Population Collapse From PCB Pollution." *Science* 361, no. 6409 (2018): 1373–76.

Global Footprint Network. "Earth Overshoot Day, 2019." Available online at www.footprintnetwork.org/our-work/earth-overshoot-day/.

Jackson, J. B. "Ecological Extinction and Evolution in the Brave New Ocean." *Proceedings of the National Academy of Sciences* 105 (2008; Suppl 1): 11458–65.

Margalef, R. *Our Biosphere*. Vol. 10 of *Excellence in Ecology*. Ecology Institute, 1997.

Seed, A., and R. Byrne. "Animal Tool-Use." *Current Biology* 20, no. 23 (2010): R1032–R1039.

Smith, C. R., A. G. Glover, T. Treude, N. D. Higgs, and D. J. Amon. "Whale-Fall Ecosystems: Recent Insights Into Ecology, Paleoecology, and Evolution." *Annual Review of Marine Science* 7 (2015): 571–96.

Teske, S., ed. *Achieving the Paris Climate Agreement Goals*. Available online at link.springer.com/content/pdf/10.1007/978-3-030-05843-2.pdf.

Worm, B., and R. T. Paine. "Humans as a Hyperkeystone Species." *Trends in Ecology & Evolution* 31, no. 8 (2016): 600–607.

CHAPTER 9: DIVERSITY IS GOOD

Cardinale, B. J., J. E. Duffy, A. Gonzalez, D. U. Hooper, C. Perrings, P. Venail, A. Narwani, et al. "Biodiversity Loss and Its Impact on Humanity." *Nature* 486, no. 7401 (2012): 59–67.

Darwin, C. *On the Origin of Species by Means of Natural Selection, or the Preservation of Favoured Races in the Struggle for Life*. John Murray, 1859.

Pauly, D., and D. Zeller. "Catch Reconstructions Reveal That Global Marine Fisheries Catches Are Higher Than Reported and Declining." *Nature Communication* 7 (2016): 10244.

Sala, E., and N. Knowlton. "Global Marine Biodiversity Trends." *Annual Review of Environment and Resources* 31 (2006): 93–122.

Wilson, E. O. *The Diversity of Life*. W. W. Norton and Company, 1999.

Worm, B., E. B. Barbier, N. Beaumont, J. E. Duffy, C. Folke, B. S. Halpern, J. B. C. Jackson, et al. "Impacts of Biodiversity Loss on Ocean Ecosystem Services." *Science* 314, no. 5800 (2006): 787–90.

Zhu, Y., H. Chen, J. Fan, Y. Wang, Y. Li, J. Chen, J. Fan, et al. "Genetic Diversity and Disease Control in Rice." *Nature* 406, no. 6797 (2000): 718.

CHAPTER 10: PROTECTED AREAS

Aburto-Oropeza, O., B. Erisman, G. R. Galland, I. Mascareñas-Osorio, E. Sala, and E. Ezcurra. "Large Recovery of Fish Biomass in a No-Take Marine Reserve." *PLoS One* 6, no. 8 (2011): e23601.

Atwood, T. B., R. M. Connolly, E. G. Ritchie, C. E. Lovelock, M. R. Heithaus, G. C. Hays, J. W. Fourqurean, and P. I. Macreadie. "Predators Help Protect Carbon Stocks in Blue Carbon Ecosystems." *Nature Climate Change* 5, no. 12 (2015): 1038.

Babcock, R. C., N. T. Shears, A. C. Alcala, N. S. Barrett, G. J. Edgar, K. D. Lafferty, T. R. McClanahan, and G. R. Russ. "Decadal Trends in Marine Reserves Reveal Differential Rates of Change in Direct and Indirect Effects." *Proceedings of the National Academy of Sciences* 107, no. 43 (2010): 18256–61.

Ban, N. C., G. G. Gurney, N. A. Marshall, C. K. Whitney, M. Mills, S. Gelcich, N. J. Bennett, et al. "Well-Being Outcomes of Marine Protected Areas." *Nature Sustainability* 2, no. 6 (2019): 524.

Dinerstein, E., C. Vynne, E. Sala, A. R. Joshi, S. Fernando, T. E. Lovejoy, J. Mayorga, et al. "A Global Deal for Nature: Guiding Principles, Milestones, and Targets." *Science Advances* 5, no. 4 (2019): eaaw2869.

Garnett, S. T., N. D. Burgess, J. E. Fa, A. Fernández-Llamazares, Z. Molnár, C. J. Robinson, J. E. M. Watson, et al. "A Spatial Overview of the Global Importance of Indigenous Lands for Conservation." *Nature Sustainability* 1 (2018): 369–74.

Guidetti, P., and E. Sala. "Community-Wide Effects of Marine Reserves in the Mediterranean Sea." *Marine Ecology Progress Series* 335 (2007): 43–56.

Haddad, N. M., L. A. Brudvig, J. Clobert, K. F. Davies, A. Gonzalez, R. D. Holt, T. E. Lovejoy, et al. "Habitat Fragmentation and Its Lasting Impact on Earth's Ecosystems." *Science Advances* 1, no. 2 (2015): e1500052.

Hansen, M. M., R. Jones, and K. Tocchini. "Shinrin-Yoku (Forest Bathing) and Nature Therapy: A State-of-the-Art Review." *International Journal of Environmental Research and Public Health* 14, no. 8 (2017): 851.

Jackson, J. B. "Reefs Since Columbus." *Coral Reefs* 16, no. 1 (1997): S23–S32.

Jackson, J. B. C., M. X. Kirby, W. H. Berger, K. A. Bjorndal, L. W. Botsford, B. J. Bourque, R. H. Bradbury, et al. "Historical Overfishing and the Recent Collapse of Coastal Ecosystems." *Science* 293, no. 5530 (2001): 629–37.

Lester, S. E., B. Halpern, K. Grorud-Colvert, J. Lubchenco, B. I. Ruttenberg, S. D. Gaines, S. Airamé, and R. R. Warner. "Biological Effects Within No-Take Marine Reserves: A Global Synthesis." *Marine Ecology Progress Series* 384 (2009): 33–46.

Lovejoy, T. E., and C. Nobre. "Amazon Tipping Point." *Science Advances* 4, no. 2 (2018): eaat2340.

McClenachan, L., F. Ferretti, and J. K. Baum. "From Archives to Conservation: Why Historical Data Are Needed to Set Baselines for Marine Animals and Ecosystems." *Conservation Letters* 5, no. 5 (2012): 349–59.

Naidoo, R., D. Gerkey, D. Hole, A. Pfaff, A. M. Ellis, C. D. Golden, D. Herrera, et al. "Evaluating the Impacts of Protected Areas on Human Well-Being Across the Developing World." *Science Advances* 5, no. 4 (2019): eaav3006.

Pandolfi, J. M., R. H. Bradbury, E. Sala, T. P. Hughes, K. A. Bjorndal, R. G. Cooke, D. McArdle, et al. "Global Trajectories of the Long-Term Decline of Coral Reef Ecosystems." *Science* 301, no. 5635 (2003): 955–62.

Pauly, D. "Anecdotes and the Shifting Baseline Syndrome of Fisheries." *Trends in Ecology & Evolution* 10, no. 10 (1995): 430.

Sala, E., C. Costello, D. Dougherty, G. Heal, K. Kelleher, J. H. Murray, A. A. Rosenberg, and R. Sumaila. "A General Business Model for Marine Reserves." *PLoS One* 8, no. 4 (2013): e58799.

Sala, E., and S. Giakoumi. "No-Take Marine

Reserves Are the Most Effective Protected Areas in the Ocean." *ICES Journal of Marine Science* 75, no. 3 (2017): 1166–68.

Sala, E., J. Lubchenco, K. Grorud-Colvert, C. Novelli, C. Roberts, and U. R. Sumaila. "Assessing Real Progress Towards Effective Ocean Protection." *Marine Policy* 91 (May 2018): 11–13.

Shears, N. T., and R. C. Babcock. "Continuing Trophic Cascade Effects After 25 Years of No-Take Marine Reserve Protection." *Marine Ecology Progress Series* 246 (2003): 1–16.

Veldhuis, M. P., M. E. Ritchie, J. O. Ogutu, T. A. Morrison, C. M. Beale, A. B. Estes, W. Mwakilema, et al. "Cross-Boundary Human Impacts Compromise the Serengeti-Mara Ecosystem." *Science* 363, no. 6434 (2019): 1424–28.

CHAPTER 11: REWILDING

Cromsigt, J. P., M. te Beest, G. I. H. Kerley, M. Landman, E. le Roux, and F. A. Smith. "Trophic Rewilding as a Climate Change Mitigation Strategy?" *Philosophical Transactions of the Royal Society B: Biological Sciences* 373, no. 1761 (2018): 20170440.

Gates, B. "The Deadliest Animal in the World." *Gates Notes* (blog), April 25, 2014. Available online at www.gatesnotes.com/ Health/Most-Lethal-Animal-Mosquito -Week?WT.mc_id=MosquitoWeek2014 _SharkWeek_tw&WT.tsrc=Twitter/.

Koel, T. M., J. L. Arnold, L. A. Baril, K. A. Gunther, D. W. Smith, J. M. Syslo, and L. M. Tronstad. "Non-native Lake Trout Induce Cascading Changes in the Yellowstone Lake Ecosystem." *Yellowstone Science* 25, no. 1 (2017): 42–50.

Mayer, A., Z. Hausfather, A. D. Jones, and W. L. Silver. "The Potential of Agricultural Land Management to Contribute to Lower Global Surface Temperatures." *Science Advances* 4, no. 8 (2018): eaaq0932.

Ripple, W. J., and R. L. Beschta. "Trophic Cascades in Yellowstone: The First 15 Years After Wolf Reintroduction." *Biological Conservation* 145, no. 1 (2011): 205–13.

Sinclair, A. R. E., and M. Norton-Griffith. *Serengeti: Dynamics of an Ecosystem.* University of Chicago Press, 1979.

Smith, D., R. O. Peterson, and D. B. Houston. "Yellowstone After Wolves." *BioScience* 53, no. 4 (2003): 330–40.

Tree, I. *Wilding: The Return of Nature to a British Farm.* Picador, 2018.

Vera, F. W. M. *Grazing Ecology and Forest History.* CABI Publishing, 2000.

CHAPTER 12: THE MORAL IMPERATIVE

Diamond, J. *Collapse: How Societies Choose to Fail or Succeed.* Penguin, 2005.

Fay, J. M., and M. Nichols. *The Last Place on Earth: With Mike Fay's African Megatransect Journals.* 2 vols. National Geographic, 2005.

Garson, J., A. Plutynski, and S. Sarkar. *The Routledge Handbook of Philosophy of Biodiversity.* Taylor and Francis, 2016.

New Zealand Parliament. "Innovative Bill Protects Whanganui River With Legal Personhood," March 28, 2017. Available online at www.parliament.nz/en/ get-involved/features/innovative-bill -protects-whanganui-river-with-legal -personhood.

Pope Francis. "Laudato Si' – Encyclical Letter, Francis." Vatican: the Holy See. Libreria Editrice Vaticana, 2015. Available online at w2.vatican.va/content/ francesco/en/encyclicals/documents/ papa-francesco_20150524_enciclica -laudato-si.html.

Safina, C. "The New Threat to Endangered Species? The Trump Administration." *New York Times,* August 13, 2019.

Tucker, M. E., and J. Grim. *Ecology and Religion.* Island Press, 2013.

———. (series eds.). Religions of the World and Ecology Series. Distributed by Harvard University Press. Further information online at fore.yale.edu/publications/ books/cswr.

Wilson, E. O. *Biophilia.* Harvard University Press, 1984.

Wilson, E. O. *The Creation: An Appeal to Save*

Key References

Life on Earth. W. W. Norton and Company, 2007.

CHAPTER 13: THE ECONOMICS OF NATURE

Aburto-Oropeza, O., I. Dominguez Guerrero, J. J. Cota-Nieto, and T. Plomozo-Lugo. "Recruitment and Ontogenetic Habitat Shifts of the Yellow Snapper *(Lutjanus argentiventris)* in the Gulf of California." *Marine Biology* 156, no. 12 (2009): 2461–72.

Aburto-Oropeza, O., E. Ezcurra, G. Danemann, V. Valdez, J. Murray, and E. Sala. "Mangroves in the Gulf of California Increase Fishery Yields." *Proceedings of the National Academy of Sciences* 105, no. 30 (2008): 10456–59.

Chong, J. "Protective Values of Mangrove and Coral Ecosystems: A Review of Methods and Evidence." International Union for Conservation of Nature, 2005.

Coady, D., I. Parry, L. Sears, and B. Shang. "How Large Are Global Fossil Fuel Subsidies?" *World Development* 91 (2017): 11–27.

Costanza, R., R. de Groot, P. Sutton, S. van der Ploeg, S. J. Anderson, I. Kubiszewski, S. Farber, and R. K. Turner. "Changes in the Global Value of Ecosystem Services." *Global Environmental Change* 26 (2014): 152–58.

Dahdouh-Guebas, F., L. P. Jayatissa, D. Di Nitto, J. O. Bosire, D. Lo Seen, N. Koedam. "How Effective Were Mangroves as a Defence Against the Recent Tsunami?" *Current Biology* 15, no. 12 (2005): R443–R447.

Foley, J. A. "Can We Feed the World and Sustain the Planet?" *Scientific American* 305, no. 5 (2011): 60–65.

Food and Agriculture Organization of the United Nations (FAO). *The State of World Fisheries and Aquaculture 2018.* FAO, 2018. Available online at www.fao.org/state-of-fisheries-aquaculture.

Goñi, R., R. Hilborn, D. Díaz, S. M. Martínez, and S. Adlerstein. "Net Contribution of Spillover From a Marine Reserve to Fishery Catches." *Marine Ecology Progress Series* 400 (2010): 233–43.

Intergovernmental Panel on Climate Change (IPCC). *Climate Change and Land: An IPCC Special Report on Climate Change, Desertification, Land Degradation, Sustainable Land Management, Food Security, and Greenhouse Gas Fluxes in Terrestrial Ecosystems.* IPCC, 2019. Available online at www.ipcc.ch/srccl-report-download-page/.

Kroodsma, D. A., J. Mayorga, T. Hochberg, N. A. Miller, K. Boerder, F. Ferretti, A. Wilson, et al. "Tracking the Global Footprint of Fisheries." *Science* 359, no. 6378 (2018): 904–08.

Kumar, P., ed. *The Economics of Ecosystems and Biodiversity: Ecological and Economic Foundations.* Earthscan, 2010.

Maekawa, M., A. Lanjouw, E. Rutagarama, and D. Sharp. "Mountain Gorilla Tourism Generating Wealth and Peace in Post-conflict Rwanda." *Natural Resources Forum* 37, no. 2 (2013): 127–37.

Marshall, D. J., S. Gaines, R. Warner, D. R. Barneche, and M. Bode. "Underestimating the Benefits of Marine Protected Areas for the Replenishment of Fished Populations." *Frontiers in Ecology and the Environment.* 17, no. 7 (2019): 407–13. doi: 10.1002/fee.2075/.

McCook, L. J., T. Ayling, M. Cappo, J. H. Choat, R. D. Evans, D. M. De Freitas, M. Heupel, et al. "Adaptive Management of the Great Barrier Reef: A Globally Significant Demonstration of the Benefits of Networks of Marine Reserves." *Proceedings of the National Academy of Sciences* 107, no. 43 (2010): 18278–85.

Sala, E., C. Costello, D. Dougherty, G. Heal, K. Kelleher, J. H. Murray, A. A. Rosenberg, and R. Sumaila. "A General Business Model for Marine Reserves." *PLoS One* 8, no. 4 (2013): e58799.

Sala, E., C. Costello, J. De Bourbon Parme, M. Fiorese, G. Heal, K. Kelleher, R. Moffitt, et al. "Fish Banks: An Economic Model to Scale Marine Conservation." *Marine Policy* 73 (2016): 154–61.

Sala, E., et al. "Reconciling Biodiversity Protection, Food Production, and Climate Change Mitigation in the Global Ocean." *Nature* (2020; forthcoming).

Sathirathai, S., and E. B. Barbier. "Valuing Mangrove Conservation in Southern Thailand." *Contemporary Economic Policy* 19, no. 2 (2011): 109–22.

Sumaila, U. R., N. Ebrahim, A. Schuhbauer, D. Skerritt, Y. Li, H. S. Kim, T. G. Mallory, V. W. L. Lam, and D. Pauly. "Updated Estimates and Analysis of Global Fisheries Subsidies." *Marine Policy* 109 (2019): 103695.

Thomas, C. C., L. Koontz, and E. Cornachione. "2018 National Park Visitor Spending Effects: Economic Contributions to Local Communities, States, and the Nation." Natural Resource Report NPS/NRSS/EQD/NRR—2019/1922. National Park Service, Fort Collins, CO, 2019.

Waldron, A., et al. *Protecting 30% of the Planet for Nature: Costs, Benefits and Economic Implications.* National Geographic Society and Wyss Campaign for Nature, 2020.

World Economic Forum. "Nature Risk Rising: Why the Crisis Engulfing Nature Matters for Business and the Economy." New Nature Economy series 1 (2020). Available online at www3.weforum.org/docs/WEF_New_Nature_Economy_Report_2020.pdf

Worm, B., E. B. Barbier, N. Beaumont, J. E. Duffy, C. Folke, B. S. Halpern, J. B. C. Jackson, et al. "Impacts of Biodiversity Loss on Ocean Ecosystem Services." *Science* 314, no. 5800 (2006): 787–90.

Yu, F., Z. Chen, X. Ren, and G. Yang. "Analysis of Historical Floods on the Yangtze River, China: Characteristics and Explanations." *Geomorphology* 113, no. 3/4 (2009): 210–16.

CHAPTER 14: WHY WE NEED THE WILD

Clay, J. "Freeze the Footprint of Food." *Nature* 475, no. 7356 (2011): 287.

Gentry, R. R., H. E. Froehlich, D. Grimm, P. Kareiva, M. Parke, M. Rust, S. D. Gaines, and B. S. Halpern. "Mapping the Global Potential for Marine Aquaculture." *Nature Ecology & Evolution* 1, no. 9 (2017): 1317.

Leopold, A. *A Sand County Almanac and Sketches Here and There.* Oxford University Press, 1949.

Lovejoy, T. E., and L. Hannah (eds.). *Biodiversity and Climate Change: Transforming the Biosphere.* Yale University Press, 2019.

Pauly, D. "Aquacalypse Now: The End of Fish." *New Republic,* September 28, 2009.

Rhodes, C. J. "The Imperative for Regenerative Agriculture." *Science Progress* 100, no. 1 (2017): 80–129.

Rockström, J., J. Williams, G. Daily, A. Noble, N. Matthews, L. Gordon, H. Wetterstrand, et al. "Sustainable Intensification of Agriculture for Human Prosperity and Global Sustainability." *Ambio* 46, no. 1 (2017): 4–17.

Rodale Institute. *Regenerative Organic Agriculture and Climate Change: A Down-to-Earth Solution to Global Warming.* Rodale Institute, 2017. Available online at rodaleinstitute.org/wp-content/uploads/rodale-white-paper.pdf.

Sala, E., and K. Rechberger. "Protecting Half the Ocean?" In *From Summits to Solutions: Innovations in Implementing the Sustainable Development Goals,* edited by R. M. Desai, H. Kato, H. Kharas, and J. W. McArthur, 239–61. Brookings Institution Press, 2018.

Springmann, M., M. Clark, D. Mason-D'Croz, K. Wiebe, B. L. Bodirsky, L. Lassaletta, W. de Vries, et al. "Options for Keeping the Food System Within Environmental Limits." *Nature* 562, no. 7728 (2018): 519.

Stern, N. *The Economics of Climate Change: The Stern Review.* Cambridge University Press, 2007.

Stuart, T. *Waste: Uncovering the Global Food Scandal.* W. W. Norton and Company, 2009.

Trisos, C. H., C. Merow, and A. L. Pigot. "The Projected Timing of Abrupt Ecological Disruption from Climate Change." *Nature* (2020). Available online at https://doi.org/10.1038/s41586-020-2189-9.

Willett, W., J. Rockström, B. Loken, M. Springmann, T. Lang, S. Vermeulen, T. Garnett, et al. "Food in the Anthropocene: The EAT-Lancet Commission on Healthy Diets From Sustainable Food Systems." *Lancet* 393, no. 10170 (2019): 447–92.

Key References

Wilson, E. O. *Half Earth: Our Planet's Fight for Life*. Knopf, 2017.

World Bank. *The Sunken Billions Revisited: Progress and Challenges in Global Marine Fisheries*. World Bank, 2017. doi: 10.1596/978-1-4648-0919-4.

Zeller, D., and D. Pauly. "Back to the Future for Fisheries, Where Will We Choose to Go?" *Global Sustainability* 2 (2019): e11. doi: 10.1017/sus.2019.8.

EPILOGUE: THE NATURE OF CORONAVIRUS

Afelt, A., R. Frutos, and C. Devaux. "Bats, Coronaviruses, and Deforestation: Toward the Emergence of Novel Infectious Diseases?" *Frontiers in Microbiology* 9 (2018): 702.

Barr, J. J., R. Auro, M. Furlan, K. L. Whiteson, M. L. Erb, J. Pogliano, A. Stotland, R. Wolkowicz, A. S. Cutting, K. S. Doran, and P. Salamon. "Bacteriophage Adhering to Mucus Provide a Non–host-derived Immunity." *Proceedings of the National Academy of Sciences* 110, no. 26 (2013): 10771–76.

Bloomfield, L. S. P., T. L. McIntosh, and E. F. Lambin. "Habitat Fragmentation, Livelihood Behaviors, and Contact Between People and Nonhuman Primates in Africa." *Landscape Ecology* 35 (2020): 985–1000. Available online at doi .org/10.1007/s10980-020-00995-w.

Boni, M. F., P. Lemey, X. Jiang, T. T. Y. Lam, B. Perry, T. Castoe, A. Rambaut, and D. L. Robertson. "Evolutionary Origins of the SARS-CoV-2 Sarbecovirus Lineage Responsible for the COVID-19 Pandemic." *bioRxiv* (2020). Available online at www.biorxiv.org/content/10.1101/2020 .03.30.015008v1.

Brook, C. E., M. Boots, K. Chandran, A. P. Dobson, C. Drosten, A. L. Graham, B. T. Grenfell, M. A. Müller, M. Ng, L. F. Wang, and A. van Leeuwen. "Accelerated Viral Dynamics in Bat Cell Lines, with Implications for Zoonotic Emergence." *eLife* 9 (2020).

Civitello, D. J., J. Cohen, H. Fatima, N. T. Halstead, J. Liriano, T. A. McMahon, C. N. Ortega, E. L. Sauer, T. Sehgal, S. Young,

and J. R. Rohr. "Biodiversity Inhibits Parasites: Broad Evidence for the Dilution Effect." *Proceedings of the National Academy of Sciences* 112, no. 28 (2015): 8667–71.

Dinsdale, E. A., O. Pantos, S. Smriga, R. A. Edwards, F. Angly, L. Wegley, M. Hatay, D. Hall, E. Brown, M. Haynes, and L. Krause. "Microbial Ecology of Four Coral Atolls in the Northern Line Islands." *PloS ONE* 3, no. 2 (2008).

Fujita, M. S., and M. D. Tuttle. "Flying Foxes (Chiroptera: Pteropodidae): Threatened Animals of Key Ecological and Economic Importance." *Conservation Biology* 5, no. 4 (1991): 455–63.

Gao, F., E. Bailes, D. L. Robertson, Y. Chen, C. M. Rodenburg, S. F. Michael, L. B. Cummins, L. O. Arthur, M. Peeters, G. M. Shaw, and P. M. Sharp. "Origin of HIV-1 in the Chimpanzee *Pan troglodytes troglodytes*." *Nature* 397, no. 6718 (1999): 436–41.

Guo, Y. R., Q. D. Cao, Z. S. Hong, Y. Y. Tan, S. D. Chen, H. J. Jin, K. S. Tan, D. Y. Wang, and Y. Yan. "The Origin, Transmission and Clinical Therapies on Coronavirus Disease 2019 (COVID-19) Outbreak—An Update on the Status." *Military Medical Research* 7, no. 1 (2020): 1–10.

Haas, A. F., M. F. Fairoz, L. W. Kelly, C. E. Nelson, E. A. Dinsdale, R. A. Edwards, S. Giles, M. Hatay, N. Hisakawa, B. Knowles, and Y. W. Lim. "Global Microbialization of Coral Reefs." *Nature Microbiology* 1, no. 6 (2016): 1–7.

Johnson, C. K., P. L. Hitchens, P. S. Pandit, J. Rushmore, T. S. Evans, C. C. W. Young, and M. M. Doyle. "Global Shifts in Mammalian Population Trends Reveal Key Predictors of Virus Spillover Risk." *Proceedings of the Royal Society B: Biological Sciences* 287 (2020): 20192736.

Lau, S. K., P. C. Woo, K. S. Li, Y. Huang, H. W. Tsoi, B. H. Wong, S. S. Wong, S. Y. Leung, K. H. Chan, and K. Y. Yuen. "Severe Acute Respiratory Syndrome Coronavirus-Like Virus in Chinese Horseshoe Bats." *Proceedings of the National Academy of Sciences* 102, no. 39 (2005): 14040–45.

Levi, T., A. M. Kilpatrick, M. Mangel, and C. C. Wilmers. "Deer, Predators, and the

Emergence of Lyme Disease." *Proceedings of the National Academy of Sciences* 109, no. 27 (2012): 10942–47.

Lu, R., X. Zhao, J. Li, P. Niu, B. Yang, H. Wu, W. Wang, H. Song, B. Huang, N. Zhu, and Y. Bi. "Genomic Characterisation and Epidemiology of 2019 Novel Coronavirus: Implications for Virus Origins and Receptor Binding." *The Lancet* 395, no. 10224 (2020): 565–74.

Mena, I., M. I. Nelson, F. Quezada-Monroy, J. Dutta, R. Cortes-Fernández, J. H. Lara-Puente, F. Castro-Peralta, L. F. Cunha, N. S. Trovão, B. Lozano-Dubernard, and A. Rambaut. "Origins of the 2009 H1N1 Influenza Pandemic in Swine in Mexico." *eLife* 5 (2016): p.e16777.

Mietzsch, M., and M. Agbandje-McKenna. "The Good That Viruses Do." *Annual Review of Virology* 4 (2017): pp. iii–v. Available online at https://doi.org/10.1146/annurev-vi-04-071217-100011.

Nellemann, C. (editor in chief); R. Henriksen, A. Kreilhuber, D. Stewart, M. Kotsovou, P. Raxter, E. Mrema, and S. Barrat (eds.). *The Rise of Environmental Crime—A Growing Threat to Natural Resources, Peace, Development and Security.* A UNEP-INTERPOL Rapid Response Assessment, United Nations Environment Programme and RHIPTO Rapid Response–Norwegian Center for Global Analyses, 2016.

Patil, R. R., C. S. Kumar, and M. Bagvandas. "Biodiversity Loss: Public Health Risk of Disease Spread and Epidemics." *Annals of Tropical Medicine and Public Health* 10, no. 6 (2017): 1432.

Quammen, David. *Spillover: Animal Infections and the Next Human Pandemic.* W. W. Norton & Company, 2012.

Sandin, S. A., J. E. Smith, E. E. DeMartini, E. A. Dinsdale, S. D. Donner, A. M. Friedlander, T. Konotchick, M. Malay, J. E. Maragos, D. Obura, and O. Pantos. "Baselines and Degradation of Coral Reefs in the Northern Line Islands." *PloS ONE* 3, no. 2 (2008).

Vezzulli, L., R. R. Colwell, and C. Pruzzo. "Ocean Warming and Spread of Pathogenic *Vibrios* in the Aquatic Environment." *Microbial Ecology* 65, no. 4 (2013): 817–25.

Waldron, A., et al. *Report on the Costs, Benefits, and Economic Implications of Protecting 30% of the Planet.* National Geographic Society and Wyss Campaign for Nature, 2020.

Wolfe, N. D., C. P. Dunavan, and J. Diamond, J. "Origins of Major Human Infectious Diseases." *Nature* 447, no. 7142 (2007): 279–83.

Wood, C. L., K. D. Lafferty, G. DeLeo, H. S. Young, P. J. Hudson, and A. M. Kuris. "Does Biodiversity Protect Humans Against Infectious Disease?" *Ecology* 95, no. 4 (2014): 817–32.

World Wildlife Fund. "The Loss of Nature and Rise of Pandemics: Protecting Human and Planetary Health." World Wildlife Fund, 2020. Available online at wwf.panda.org/?361716.

Zhang, Z., Q. Wu, and T. Zhang. "Pangolin Homology Associated with 2019-nCoV." *bioRxiv* (2020). Available online at doi.org/10.1101/2020.02.19.950253.

INDEX

A

Aburto, Octavio 149, 195–196
Acropora corals 59
Adriatic Sea 37
Agriculture
  benefits of crop diversity
    139–140
  and biodiversity loss
    15–16, 205–206, 212
  freshwater use 115, 215
  government subsidies
    205–206, 215
  land use 16, 115, 214
  monocultures 16, 61–62,
    71, 115, 139–141, 204,
    215
  nutrient runoff 92, 101,
    215
  regenerative practices
    101, 172, 216
  soil degradation 101, 157,
    203, 215
Air pollution 147, 206. *see
  also* Carbon pollution
Alaska
  gray whales 67–68
  orcas 85, 87–88
  sea otters 85–88
  sea urchins 86, 88, 89
Algae
  algal blooms 63, 92–93,
    135
  algal communities 20–21,
    27
  algal forests 27, 89, 90,
    145, 149

biodiversity 20, 90
  microscopic 58, 63, 65,
    106, 174
  oxygen production 58,
    204
  types of 20
Alpatov, Vladimir 34
Amazon Basin, South
  America
  dust from Sahara 106
  forest biodiversity 51
  illegal cutting and
    burning 160
  indigenous peoples 73,
    104–105, 160
  rain and weather
    patterns 105, 153–154
Andes, South America 105
Antarctica
  migratory birds 68
  pollution 82–83
Apex predators 164–165
Aquaculture 217
Archaea 15, 188
Atacama Desert, Chile 51–52

B

Bacteria
  gut bacteria 107–108
  in the ocean 58, 63, 96–
    97, 124, 204, 232–234
  oxygen production 58,
    96–97, 204
  pathogens 227, 232, 238
  photosynthesis 63, 96–97,
    232

role in decomposition 57,
    123, 124
  in soil 99–100, 106
  species numbers 15
Bacteriophages 237–238
Baja California, Mexico 68,
    148, 195
Ballesteros, Enric 20, 26
Bats 13, 203, 224–227, 235,
    236
Beef production 214
Bialowieza Forest, Poland-
  Belarus 210
Biodiversity
  benefits of 129–141, 159,
    207
  conservation efforts 141,
    151, 159, 192, 206, 207
  global heating as threat
    126, 217–218
  and human health 224,
    236
  measures of 131–133
  question of importance
    130–134, 137, 140
  value of 188–189
Biodiversity loss
  marine 115, 138, 158–159,
    216
  terrestrial 15–16, 115, 158,
    205–206, 212
Biophilia 180, 183
Biosphere 2, Oracle, Ariz.
    11–14, 16, 17
Blue whales 97, 118
Bongo Ondimba, Ali 185–187

Borneo 71, 115, 155, 225
Bottom trawling 150, 159, 208
Boudouresque, Charles-François 25
Bromeliads 54
Brown algae 20, 22, 27, 90, 92–93
Burrell, Charlie 167–173

C
Cabo Pulmo, Mexico 148–149, 201
California, Gulf of 148–149, 195
Carbon pollution 57, 101, 126, 159, 211, 216
Carbon sequestration 57, 101, 156, 159, 166, 196, 216
Caribbean Sea 59, 91–93, 148, 198
Carr, Greg 157
Chernobyl disaster (1986) 31
Chimpanzees 119, 228, 234, 236
Cintu, Monte, Corsica, France 27, 28
Circular economy 57–58, 124, 238
Cities: as ecosystems 30–31, 74–75, 125
Civets 226, 235, 236
Climate change mitigation
dietary shifts 214–215
economics of 219
expanding protected areas 159–160, 208
fossil fuel phaseout 218
reducing food waste 213–214
regenerative agriculture 101, 172, 216
rewilding 166
Columbretes Islands Marine Reserve, Spain 197–198
Columbus, Christopher 147
Competitive exclusion principle 41–42
Congo, Democratic Republic of the 199, 234
Congo Basin, Africa 211, 228
Convention on Biological Diversity (CBD) 221

Copepods 174, 175
Coral reefs
algae overgrowth 22, 92–93
biodiversity 45, 132, 133, 236
development of 47–49
ecological succession 54, 56, 59, 67, 111–112
fossil record 59
human impact on 231–234
and lava flows 47–50, 60
pathogens 232–234, 236
pioneer species 48, 49, 59
pristine 91, 111–112, 132
shark numbers 91, 111–112, 132, 232
Coronavirus, novel (SARS-CoV-2) 23–24, 223–225, 234
Corsica (island), France 25–28, 32, 69, 133
Costa Brava, Catalonia, Spain 18, 89, 144
Cousteau, Jacques 143–145
COVID-19 23–24, 223–224, 235–237
Cows: methane production 214
Cutthroat trout 174–176

D
D'Ancona, Umberto 36–37
Darwin, Charles 35–36, 119
Davis, Wade 73
Dayton, Paul 82–83, 88, 93
Diadema antillarum 92–93
Diatoms 63, 105–106
Didinium nasutum 42–45
Dietary shifts 214–215
Dolphins 64, 118, 119–120, 144
Dugongs 155

E
Ecological succession, process of 50–62, 67, 115–116
Ecotourism 157, 200–202
Eleonora's falcons 69
England: rewilding 167–172

Estes, Jim 85–88, 93
Estuarine ecosystems 134–135
Ethanol 39, 40
European bison 168–169, 210
Evapotranspiration 58, 105
Exponential growth 35–36
Extinct species 15, 112–113, 120, 158, 229

F
Fay, J. Michael 185
Fermentation 39
Fisheries 134–138, 146, 151, 192, 207, 216–217
Food production 17, 197, 212–216
Food waste 213–214
Forests
ancient 50–51, 209–210
ecological succession 50–58
evapotranspiration 58, 105
forest fires 51, 60, 165
forest therapy 156
fragmentation 158, 166
mycorrhizal networks 103–104
tropical 55, 71, 115, 166, 202, 218, 226, 228
see also Mangrove forests; Rainforests
Fossil fuels 70, 121, 125–126, 206, 218, 219, 238
Fossils 59
Foundation species 83–84, 92, 93, 97, 104
Foxes 30, 123, 163, 229–230
Francis, Pope 181–182
Fungi 51–57, 100–104, 123, 171

G
Gabon 117, 185–187, 211, 220
Garrabou, Joaquim 26
Gause, Georgyi Frantsevich 33–45, 49, 55, 80
Geometric growth 35–36
Giakoumi, Sylvaine 150
Giant clams 233–234

Index

Giant kelps 83–84
Giraffes 113, 165
Girona, University of,
  Girona, Spain 18, 19
Global heating 73–74, 163–
  166, 172, 206, 217–219
Glomalin 101, 171
Gomantong Caves, Borneo
  225
Goodall, Jane 119
Gorongosa National Park,
  Mozambique 157–158
Grasslands 16, 91, 153, 157–
  158, 203, 214, 215
Gray whales 67–68, 123–124
Great Barrier Reef Marine
  Park, Australia 201
Green algae 20
Green turtles 148
Greenhouse gas emissions
  126, 207, 213–215
Grigg, Richard 47–48
Gross domestic product
  (GDP) 72, 76, 194, 204–
  205, 219
Groupers 144, 145, 146, 149,
  185, 187
Gut bacteria 107–108

H
Habitat destruction 115–116,
  158–159, 236
Hatfield, Brian 87
Hawaii 47–49, 50, 67
Horseshoe bats 224
Humpback whales 30, 68,
  117, 118–119

I
Indigenous peoples 73, 96,
  160, 182–183
Influenza pandemic (2009)
  230
International Space Station
  (ISS) 16–17, 32, 95, 109
Intertidal zone 78–82, 84, 85
Iron 97–98, 105, 106

J
Jackson, Jeremy 147–148

K
Kelp forests 83–86, 88, 144
Keystone predators 86, 87,
  92, 113, 118, 176, 229
Kibale National Park,
  Uganda 228
Kilauea volcano, Hawaii 47
Killer whales. *see* Orcas
Kingman Reef, Line Islands,
  Pacific Ocean 91, 231–233
Knepp (farm), West Sussex,
  England 167–172
Krill 97–98, 118

L
Lake trout 174–176
Lava flows 47–50, 60
Leopold, Aldo 220–221
Livestock diseases 165, 230
Livestock production
  animal feed 214
  impact on biodiversity
    15–16, 115, 214, 228
  land use 16, 115, 214
  overgrazing and soil
    degradation 157, 203
Loder, Natasha 129–130, 131,
  140
Logistic growth 34
Long-spine sea urchins
  92–93
Lotka, Alfred 42
Lotka-Volterra equations
  42–43, 44
Lovejoy, Tom 217
Lyme disease 229–230
Lynx-hare dynamic 43–45,
  112, 113, 120

M
Macron, Emmanuel 209
Mangrove forests 60, 131,
  194–197
Maori tribes 183
Margalef, Ramón 53–54, 56,
  122–123
Marine reserves 138, 148–
  151, 157, 187, 197–201, 216
Marshes 134
McClenachan, Loren 148
McMurdo Station,
  Antarctica 82

Medes Islands Marine
  Reserve, Spain 89–91,
  123, 145–146, 148, 200–
  201
Mediterranean monk seals
  112–113
Mediterranean Sea
  algae 18, 20–21, 90–91
  sea urchins 90–91, 149–
    150
  spiny lobsters 146, 198
  trophic cascades 90,
    149–150
  see also Columbretes
    Islands Marine
    Reserve; Medes
    Islands Marine
    Reserve
Mexico
  flu outbreak (2009) 230
  mangrove forests 195–196
  marine protected areas
    148–149, 193, 201
  tuna fishing industry 193
Microcosms, experimental
  36, 38–44
Midwest (region), U.S. 16, 75,
  115
Migrations, animal 67–69
Millennium Atoll, Line
  Islands, Pacific Ocean
  111, 233
Monocultures 16, 61–62, 71,
  115, 139–141, 204, 215
Mountain gorillas 199–200,
  234
Mushrooms, wild 27, 28, 51,
  52
Mycorrhizae 100, 103–104

N
National Center for
  Ecological Analysis and
  Synthesis (NCEAS) 130–
  131, 133
National Geographic
  Society 111, 184, 191, 206,
  221, 233
Necrosphere 123–127, 163,
  211–212
New York City, N.Y. 30–31,
  60–61, 74–75, 93–94, 133,
  234

Noise pollution 117–118
Nôtre-Dame Cathedral,
   Paris, France 209, 210

O
Oceans
   acoustic pollution 117–
      118
   biodiversity loss 115, 138,
      158–159, 216
   dead zones 101, 215
   ecotourism 200–201
   overfishing 114, 158–159,
      216–217
   protected areas 138, 148–
      151, 157, 187, 197–201,
      216
   viruses and bacteria 58,
      63, 96–97, 124, 204,
      232–234
   see also Coral reefs
Ochre sea stars. see Pisaster
   ochraceus
Odum, Eugene 53–54
Oil drilling 117–118, 191
Oil palms 71, 115
Orcas 85, 87–88, 98, 116, 123
Otter-orca phenomenon
   87–88, 116
Overfishing 22, 92, 132, 205,
   216–217
Oxygen, atmospheric 57, 58,
   131, 204–205

P
Paine, Robert T. 77–82, 85–
   88, 93, 94, 113, 118
Palm oil plantations 71, 115
Pandemics 23–24, 223–238
Pandolfi, John 59
Pangolins 225–226, 235, 236
Paramecium 38–39, 41–44,
   80
Paris Climate Agreement
   126, 160, 172
Pauly, Daniel 136, 146, 220
Pesticides 101, 167, 168, 170,
   204, 215
Photosynthesis 56–57, 63,
   96–98, 121, 155, 156, 232
Phytoplankton 63–66, 91,
   97–98, 105–106, 174–176

Pioneer species 48, 49, 52–
   53, 59
Pisaster ochraceus 78–81,
   84, 113
Plagues 227, 237
Plan B (research vessel)
   185–186
Plankton 65, 67, 68, 73, 79
Plant-based diet 214–215
Plant biomass 121–122, 125,
   134
Plants
   carbon sequestration 57
   photosynthesis 56–57,
      96–98, 121, 155, 156
   and soil ecosystem 99–
      101
   symbiosis with fungi 52,
      100, 103–104
Pollinators 12–13, 17, 94,
   203–204, 224
Polo, Lluís 18, 19, 20
Polychlorinated biphenyls
   (PCBs) 116
Population growth 34, 120
Predator-prey equations. see
   Lotka-Volterra equations
Pristine Seas project 22, 111,
   117, 184–187
Prochlorococcus 96–97, 232

Q
Quammen, David 226

R
Rainforests 115, 160, 166, 185
Rechberger, Kristin 199
Red algae 20, 84, 90
Red deer 169
Red foxes 30, 123, 229
Regenerative agriculture
   101, 172, 216
Religions, world 180–182
Remotely operated vehicles
   (ROVs) 186
Retezat Mountains,
   Romania 210
Revillagigedo Islands,
   Pacific Ocean 193
Rice growing 139–140
Rinderpest 165
River otters 175

Rohwer, Forest 232–233
Roosevelt, Theodore 173–
   174
Royal, Ségolène 188

S
Safina, Carl 182
Sahara, Africa 32, 106
Salema porgies 20, 28
Sand grains 105, 106
Sardines 64–67, 70, 105, 114
SARS (severe acute
   respiratory syndrome)
   224, 226
Scandola Marine Reserve,
   Corsica, France 26
Scripps Institution of
   Oceanography, La Jolla,
   Calif. 21, 67, 77, 83, 195
Sea breams 21, 145, 149
Sea otters 85–88, 92, 116, 119
Sea stars 78–81, 84, 113
Sea turtles 147, 148, 155, 185
Sea urchins 28, 79, 84–93,
   119, 144, 149
Seagrass beds 91, 146, 155–
   156
Serengeti National Park,
   Tanzania 152, 165–166,
   173
Shark Bay, Australia 119,
   155–156, 163
Sharks
   abundance in protected
      areas 149, 150
   as keystone species 92
   in overfished coral reefs
      132, 231–232
   predation 44, 91, 111–112,
      155–156
   in pristine coral reefs 91,
      111–112, 132, 233
Shemya Island, Alaska 86,
   89
Shinrin-yoku 156
Shrimp farms 60, 195–197
Silica 63, 105, 106
Simard, Suzanne 101–104
Smith, Fred 77–78, 85
Snappers 117, 149, 195
Soil, healthy 99–101, 216
Soil degradation 101, 157,
   203, 215

Index

Solar energy 120–121, 122, 125, 126
South Africa: sardine run 63–65, 66, 67, 105
Species, number of 14–15
Sperm whales 97, 98
Spiny lobsters 146, 198
Springer, Alan 87
Stern, Nicholas 219
The Struggle for Existence (Gause) 33
Swine flu 230

T
Thailand 197
Tiger sharks 155–156, 163
Tijuana River National Estuarine Research Reserve, Calif. 134
Tinker, Tim 87
Tool-using animals 119–120
Tourism 138, 157, 191, 199–202
Tree, Isabella 167–173
Trees
    ancient 50–51, 209–210
    carbon storage 155, 166, 211
    communication between 102–104
    human health benefits 156
    mangroves 60, 131, 194–197
    oil palms 71, 115
    Yanomami legend 104–105
Tuna fishing industry 193

U
Uganda
    human–wildlife conflict 228
    protected forests 199, 227–228
Urban ecosystems 30–31, 74–75, 125

V
Vibrio 232–234
Virunga National Park, Democratic Republic of the Congo 234

Viruses 23–24, 223–230, 234–238
Volcanoes 47–48, 197, 199
Volcanoes National Park, Rwanda 199–200, 234
Volterra, Vito 37, 42

W
Waitt, Ted 185
Waldron, Anthony 236
Washington: intertidal studies 78–82, 85
Water pollution 101, 197, 212, 217
Weeds 48, 51, 52, 56
Wet markets 223, 226–227, 237
Whales
    ecosystem role 97–98
    and sardine run 64–65
    whale fall succession 123–124
    whale songs 117, 118, 185
    see also Blue whales; Gray whales; Humpback whales
Whaling 87–88, 97, 98, 116
Whanganui River, New Zealand 183
White, Lee 185, 211
Wildebeests 36, 152, 153, 155, 165
Wildflowers 51–52, 168, 180
Wildlife trade, illegal 225, 228, 236, 238
Wilson, Edward O. 180
Wolves 44, 91, 92, 119, 153, 161–164, 229
Worm, Boris 113, 130
Wuhan, China 223

Y
Yangtze River, China: floods (1998) 202–203
Yanomami people 104–105
Yeast 38–41
Yellowstone Lake, Wyo. 174–176
Yellowstone National Park, Wyo. 119, 152, 153, 161–166, 174, 201
Yunnan Province, China: rice study 139–140

Z
Zabala, Mikel 26
Zhu Youyong 139
Zoonotic diseases 224, 227, 229-230, 235
Zooplankton 64, 65, 91

NATIONAL GEOGRAPHIC

THE NATIONAL GEOGRAPHIC SOCIETY INVESTS IN BOLD PEOPLE AND TRANSFORMATIVE IDEAS TO ILLUMINATE AND PROTECT THE WONDER OF OUR WORLD.

Scientists and conservationists, including National Geographic Explorer-in-Residence Enric Sala, have made it clear that to prevent a global extinction crisis, we must conserve at least half of the planet in its natural state.

As a key milestone, the National Geographic Society is working to support the protection of at least 30 percent of the planet by 2030. Toward that goal, the Society has partnered with the Wyss Campaign for Nature to launch the Campaign for Nature, a global effort to raise awareness about the urgent need to protect nature and enable people and wildlife to thrive.

Together we can protect these places—and the people that depend on them—before it's too late.

ABOUT THE NATIONAL GEOGRAPHIC SOCIETY

The National Geographic Society is a global nonprofit organization that uses the power of science, exploration, education, and storytelling to illuminate and protect the wonder of the world. Since 1888, National Geographic has pushed the boundaries of exploration, investing in bold people and transformative ideas, providing more than 14,000 grants for work across all seven continents, reaching three million students each year through education offerings, and engaging audiences around the globe through signature experiences, stories, and content. To learn more, visit www.nationalgeographic.org or follow us on Instagram, Twitter, and Facebook.